SPICE IT UP!

Publications International, Ltd.

Microwave Cooking: Microwave ovens vary in wattage. Use the cooking times as guidelines and check for doneness before adding more time.

CONTENTS

SPICE IT UP!

It's hard to imagine a world without spice—not only would our food be unbearably bland, but the world would be a vastly different place! The search for spices led to discoveries of new lands and new foods, changing the course of history through colonizations, wars and political upheavals. Fortunately those dangerous days are long gone; we now enjoy exotic herbs and spices and the cuisines of other countries in the comfort of our own kitchens.

So what's the difference between herbs and spices? Herbs are the leaves of fresh or dried herbaceous plants (plants with stems that are soft rather than woody), while spices are the aromatic parts of plants, such as bark, berries, buds, flowers, fruit, roots or seeds. Spices come from plants that thrive in tropical regions, while herbs are outdoor plants that can grow places besides the tropics. The categories can overlap at times, because a plant can provide both an herb and a spice—for example, fresh cilantro leaves, coriander seeds and dried ground coriander all come from the coriander plant. The classifications may be a little confusing, but the primary purpose of herbs and spices is the same—to accent and enhance the flavor of foods.

AVAILABILITY

Fresh herbs for cooking have become increasingly popular in recent years. Some of the more common fresh herbs, such as basil, chives, dill, mint, oregano, rosemary, sage, tarragon and thyme, are available year-round in large supermarkets. They can be found either cut or potted, and most can be easily grown in the home garden. Dried herbs and spices, both leaf and herb form, are readily available all year in any supermarket.

STORAGE

fresh

Fresh herbs are very perishable, so purchase them in small amounts. Place the stems in water, cover the leaves loosely with a plastic bag or plastic wrap and store them in the refrigerator. They will last from two days (basil, chives, dill, mint, oregano) to five days (rosemary, sage, tarragon, thyme).

Freezing can extend the life of fresh herbs with a minimal loss of flavor. Simply clean the herbs and seal them in 2- or 3-tablespoon quantities in freezer bags, either alone or in favorite combinations. Label the bags and store them in a protective container to prevent damage to the herbs. Another option is to chop the herbs finely, half-fill ice cube tray compartments with the chopped herbs, fill with water and then freeze. Remove the cubes and store them in freezer bags; they can be used to flavor individual dishes.

dried

To preserve their flavor and color, store dried herbs and spices in a cool, dry place, away from sources of light, heat or moisture. Avoid storing them too close to the stove, oven, dishwasher or refrigerator even if those are the most convenient places, as the steam and heat produced by these appliances will rapidly diminish the flavors.

SPICE IT UP!

To protect against moisture, store dried herbs and spices in airtight containers (glass jars, plastic containers, tins, etc.). Dark glass or pottery jars work well to protect herbs and spices from exposure to light, which makes them deteriorate more quickly. If you use clear glass or plastic containers, store them inside kitchen cabinets.

SHELF LIFE

Since dried herbs and spices lose their color, taste and aroma over time, it's a good idea to purchase them in small quantities and try to use them within six months. To ensure freshness, check your dried herbs and spices at least twice a year and use your senses to judge.

• *First, test the aroma.* When you crush a small amount of the herb or spice in your hand, does it smell rich and full or has it lost most of its potency? If you have a freshly purchased jar, compare the aromas between the new and old to note the difference.

• *Next, look at the color.* Leafy green herbs will fade upon aging (although different herbs vary naturally in color and shouldn't be compared against each other). Red spices, such as red pepper, chili powder and paprika, will turn from red to brown with age. Refrigerating your red spices will help prevent loss of color and flavor, and is also recommended in hot climates to prevent infestation.

COOKING WITH HERBS & SPICES

fresh

Fresh herbs lose a great deal of their flavor when heated, so it's best to add them to a dish near the end of its cooking time. If this is not possible, try stirring in a few tablespoons of chopped herbs just before serving to perk up the flavor. However, for uncooked foods, such as salads and dressings, fresh herbs should be added several hours before serving to allow the flavors to blend.

dried

Dried herbs and spices should generally be added near the beginning of cooking to allow the flavors to develop. You can intensify the flavor of dried herbs somewhat by crushing them in your hand before adding them to a dish; this helps release the herbs' aromatic oils. To bring out the flavor and aroma of spices, such as cumin, coriander, fennel seeds or sesame seeds, toast them before using. Simply heat a heavy skillet over medium heat until hot, add the spices and cook until they are fragrant and lightly browned, stirring constantly to prevent burning.

Many herb-and-spice blends are currently available in the supermarket and are a convenient way to add new flavors to your cooking. Some blends are quite common, such as Italian seasoning, chili powder, Chinese five-spice powder and pumpkin pie spice, while others are classic combinations better known in other cultures and their cuisines.

Bouquets garnis are the little bundles of aromatic herbs and spices used to flavor soups, stews and sauces. Traditionally bouquets garnis contain parsley, thyme and bay leaf; the herbs are either tied together or placed in a cheesecloth bag for easy removal before a dish is served.

Fines herbes are a combination of chervil, chives, parsley and tarragon; this blend is finely chopped and added to a dish shortly before serving.

Herbes de Provence is an assortment of dried herbs commonly used in southern France, often containing basil, fennel seed, lavender, marjoram, rosemary, sage, summer savory and thyme.

Quatre épices literally means "four spices" and is a combination of any of the following: pepper, nutmeg, ginger, cinnamon or cloves. This mixture is used to flavor soups, stews and vegetables.

BASIL

Basil Chicken and Vegetables on Focaccia

½ **cup mayonnaise**
¼ **teaspoon garlic powder**
½ **teaspoon black pepper, divided**
1 **loaf (16 ounces) focaccia or Italian bread**
4 **boneless skinless chicken breast halves (about 1¼ pounds)**
3 **tablespoons olive oil**
2 **cloves garlic, minced**
1½ **teaspoons dried basil leaves**
½ **teaspoon salt**
1 **green bell pepper, stemmed, seeded and cut into quarters**
1 **medium zucchini, cut lengthwise into 4 slices**
2 **Italian plum tomatoes, sliced**

Combine mayonnaise, garlic powder and ¼ teaspoon black pepper in small bowl; set aside.

Cut focaccia into quarters. Cut each quarter horizontally in half; set aside.

Combine chicken, oil, garlic, basil, salt and remaining ¼ teaspoon black pepper in large resealable plastic food storage bag. Seal bag; knead to combine. Add bell pepper and zucchini; knead to coat.

Grill or broil chicken, bell pepper and zucchini 4 inches from heat source 6 to 8 minutes on each side or until chicken is no longer pink in center. (Bell pepper and zucchini may take less time.)

Top bottom half of each focaccia quarter with mayonnaise mixture, tomatoes, bell pepper, zucchini and chicken. Top with focaccia tops.

Makes 4 servings

Basil Chicken and Vegetables on Focaccia

11

BASIL

spice note

Basil, also called sweet basil, is a member of the mint family. Over 150 different varieties of basil are grown, including less common varieties like purple ruffle, lemon basil and cinnamon basil.

Mediterranean-Style Roasted Vegetables

1½ **pounds red potatoes**
  1 **tablespoon plus 1½ teaspoons olive oil, divided**
  1 **red bell pepper**
  1 **yellow or orange bell pepper**
  1 **small red onion**
  2 **cloves garlic, minced**
  ½ **teaspoon salt**
  ¼ **teaspoon black pepper**
  1 **tablespoon balsamic vinegar**
  ¼ **cup chopped fresh basil leaves**

1. Preheat oven to 425°F. Spray large shallow metal roasting pan with nonstick cooking spray. Cut potatoes into 1½-inch chunks; place in pan. Drizzle 1 tablespoon oil over potatoes; toss to coat. Bake 10 minutes.

2. Cut bell peppers into 1½-inch chunks. Cut onion through core into ½-inch wedges. Add bell peppers and onion to pan. Drizzle remaining 1½ teaspoons oil over vegetables; sprinkle with garlic, salt and black pepper. Toss well to coat. Return to oven; bake 18 to 20 minutes or until vegetables are brown and tender, stirring once.

3. Transfer to large serving bowl. Drizzle vinegar over vegetables; toss to coat. Add basil; toss again. Serve warm or at room temperature with additional black pepper, if desired. *Makes 6 servings*

Tomato Basil Dressing

  ½ **cup tomato juice**
  3 **tablespoons red wine vinegar***
  2 **tablespoons scallions, chopped**
  1 **tablespoon lemon juice**
  1 **tablespoon sugar**
  1 **teaspoon dried oregano leaves**
  ½ **teaspoon dried basil leaves**

**For more tomato taste, use only 2 tablespoons vinegar.*

Combine all ingredients in jar with tight-fitting lid. Cover and shake vigorously. Chill or serve immediately over green salad or pasta salad. *Makes 4 servings*

Favorite recipe from **The Sugar Association, Inc.**

Mediterranean-Style Roasted Vegetables

13

BASIL

Pizzette with Basil

1 can (6 ounces) CONTADINA® Italian Paste with Italian Seasonings
2 tablespoons softened cream cheese
2 tablespoons chopped fresh basil or 2 teaspoons dried basil leaves
1 loaf (1 pound) Italian bread, sliced ¼ inch thick
8 ounces mozzarella cheese, thinly sliced
Whole basil leaves (optional)
Freshly ground black pepper (optional)

1. Combine tomato paste, cream cheese and chopped basil in small bowl.

2. Toast bread slices on *ungreased* baking sheet under broiler, 6 to 8 inches from heat, turning after 1 minute, until lightly browned on both sides; remove from broiler.

3. Spread 2 teaspoons tomato mixture onto each toasted bread slice; top with 1 slice (about ¼ ounce) mozzarella cheese.

4. Broil 6 to 8 inches from heat for 1 to 2 minutes or until cheese begins to melt. Top with whole basil leaves and pepper, if desired.

Makes about 30 pizzas

Pasta, Chicken & Broccoli Pesto Toss

4 ounces (about 2 cups) uncooked vegetable spiral pasta
2 cups cubed, cooked chicken or turkey breast meat
2 cups small broccoli florets, cooked crisp-tender, cooled
1½ cups (6 ounces) SARGENTO® Light Shredded Mozzarella Cheese
⅔ cup lightly packed fresh basil leaves
2 cloves garlic
1 cup mayonnaise
1 tablespoon lemon juice
½ teaspoon salt
½ cup (1½ ounces) SARGENTO® Shredded Parmesan Cheese
½ cup pine nuts or coarsely chopped walnuts, toasted

Cook pasta according to package directions until tender; drain and cool. Combine pasta, chicken, broccoli and Mozzarella cheese in large bowl. Blend basil and garlic in covered blender or food processor until finely chopped. Add mayonnaise, lemon juice and salt. Process to combine thoroughly. Stir in Parmesan cheese. Add to pasta mixture; toss to coat well. Stir in pine nuts. Serve immediately or cover and refrigerate. For maximum flavor, remove from refrigerator 30 minutes before serving. *Makes 8 servings*

Pizzette with Basil

BASIL

Ham and Cheese Calzones

  1 pound frozen bread dough, thawed
  1 cup bottled marinara sauce
  2 tablespoons low-sodium tomato paste
  1 tablespoon slivered fresh basil leaves or 1 teaspoon dried basil
  1 cup (4 ounces) slivered ALPINE LACE® Boneless Cooked Ham
1½ cups (6 ounces) shredded ALPINE LACE® Fat Free Pasteurized
      Process Skim Milk Cheese Product—For Mozzarella Lovers
  1 cup cooked small broccoli florets, drained
  ½ cup finely chopped red onion

1. Preheat the oven to 425°F. Spray 2 baking sheets with nonstick cooking spray. On a lightly floured surface, cut the dough into 6 equal pieces. Roll each piece into a 6-inch circle.

2. In a small bowl, blend the marinara sauce with the tomato paste and basil. Leaving a ½-inch border, spread the sauce over half of each dough circle. Then sprinkle with the ham, cheese and vegetables.

3. Moisten the edges of the dough with a little water, fold the dough over filling and seal with a fork. Place on the baking sheets. Bake at 450°F for 10 minutes. Serve hot! *Makes 6 calzones*

Tomato, Basil & Broccoli Chicken

  4 skinless, boneless chicken breast halves
    Salt and black pepper (optional)
  2 tablespoons margarine or butter
  1 package (6.9 ounces) RICE-A-RONI® Chicken Flavor
  1 teaspoon dried basil leaves
  2 cups broccoli florets
  1 medium tomato, seeded, chopped
  1 cup (4 ounces) shredded mozzarella cheese

1. Sprinkle chicken with salt and pepper, if desired.

2. In large skillet, melt margarine over medium-high heat. Add chicken; cook 2 minutes on each side or until browned. Remove from skillet; set aside, reserving drippings. Keep warm.

3. In same skillet, sauté rice-vermicelli mix in reserved drippings over medium heat until vermicelli is golden brown. Stir in 2½ cups water, contents of seasoning packet and basil. Place chicken over rice mixture; bring to a boil over high heat.

4. Cover; reduce heat. Simmer 15 minutes. Top with broccoli and tomato.

5. Cover; continue to simmer 5 minutes or until liquid is absorbed and chicken is no longer pink in center. Sprinkle with cheese. Cover; let stand a few minutes before serving.

Makes 4 servings

Last Minute Tomato Swirl Bread

2 loaves (16 ounces each) frozen bread dough, thawed according to package directions
2 large cloves garlic, pressed
1 jar (8 ounces) SONOMA® Marinated Tomatoes, drained and blotted with paper towels
3 tablespoons grated Parmesan cheese
2 tablespoons dried basil leaves
Cornmeal for baking sheets
1 egg, beaten

Preheat oven to 400°F. On lightly floured surface, roll and pat one loaf of dough into 12×7-inch rectangle. Gently sprinkle half of garlic over dough. Distribute half of tomatoes evenly over dough, leaving ½-inch border. Sprinkle with half of cheese and basil. Starting from one long edge, roll dough up tightly, jelly-roll style. Carefully pinch seam to seal. Repeat procedure with second loaf. Sprinkle baking sheets with cornmeal. Place loaves on baking sheets, seam sides down. Brush with egg. Do not let rise. Bake immediately 25 to 30 minutes or until loaves are browned and sound hollow when tapped. Remove to racks to cool before slicing. If desired, loaves can be wrapped well and frozen up to 1 month.

Makes 2 loaves (24 slices)

Tip: *The flavorful oil from Marinated Tomatoes can be used for sautéing or for vinaigrettes.*

Herbed Vinegar

1½ cups white wine vinegar
½ cup fresh basil leaves

Pour vinegar into nonaluminum 2-quart saucepan. Heat until very hot, stirring occasionally. Do not boil. (If vinegar boils, it will become cloudy.)

Pour into glass bowl; add basil. Cover with plastic wrap. Let stand in cool place about 1 week until desired amount of flavor develops. Strain before using. Store up to 6 months in jar or bottle with tight-fitting lid.

Makes about 1½ cups vinegar

Variation: *Substitute 1 tablespoon of either fresh oregano, thyme, chervil or tarragon for the basil. Or, substitute cider vinegar for the wine vinegar.*

BASIL

Classic Pesto with Linguine

- ¾ **pound uncooked linguine**
- 2 **tablespoons butter or margarine**
- ¼ **cup plus 1 tablespoon olive oil, divided**
- 2 **tablespoons pine nuts**
- 1 **cup tightly packed fresh (not dried) basil leaves, rinsed, drained and stemmed**
- 2 **cloves garlic**
- ¼ **teaspoon salt**
- ¼ **cup freshly grated Parmesan cheese**
- 1½ **tablespoons freshly grated Romano cheese**
   Fresh basil leaves for garnish

1. Prepare linguine according to package directions; drain. Toss with butter in large serving bowl; set aside and keep warm.

2. Heat 1 tablespoon oil in small saucepan or skillet over medium-low heat. Add pine nuts; cook and stir 30 to 45 seconds until light brown, shaking pan constantly. Remove with slotted spoon; drain on paper towels.

3. Place toasted pine nuts, basil leaves, garlic and salt in food processor or blender. With processor running, add remaining ¼ cup oil in slow steady stream until evenly blended and pine nuts are finely chopped.

4. Transfer basil mixture to small bowl. Stir in Parmesan and Romano cheeses.*

5. Combine hot, buttered linguine and pesto sauce in large serving bowl; toss until well coated. Garnish, if desired. Serve immediately.

Makes 4 servings (about ¾ cup pesto sauce)

Pesto sauce can be stored at this point in airtight container; pour thin layer of olive oil over pesto and cover. Refrigerate up to 1 week. Bring to room temperature. Proceed as directed in step 5.

Classic Pesto with Linguine

19

BASIL

Tomato, Potato and Basil Skillet

1 tablespoon olive oil, divided
3 cups sliced potatoes
1/3 cup minced fresh basil
2 whole eggs
2 egg whites
2 tablespoons skim milk
1 tablespoon Dijon mustard
1 teaspoon dry mustard
1/2 teaspoon salt
1/4 teaspoon freshly ground pepper
2 cups sliced plum tomatoes

1. Heat 1½ teaspoons oil in medium nonstick skillet over medium heat until hot. Layer half of potato slices in skillet. Cover and cook 3 minutes or until lightly browned. Turn potatoes and cook, covered, 3 minutes or until lightly browned. Remove potatoes from skillet. Repeat with remaining 1½ teaspoons oil and potatoes.

2. Arrange all potatoes in skillet. Sprinkle with basil. Whisk together eggs, egg whites, milk, mustards, salt and pepper in small bowl. Pour over potatoes. Arrange tomatoes over potato mixture. Reduce heat to low. Cover and cook 10 minutes or until eggs are set.   *Makes 4 servings*

Stuffed Portobello Mushrooms

4 portobello mushrooms (4 ounces each)
1/4 cup olive oil
2 cloves garlic, pressed
6 ounces crumbled goat cheese
2 ounces prosciutto or thinly sliced ham, chopped
1/4 cup chopped fresh basil
Mixed salad greens

Remove stems and gently scrape gills from underside of mushrooms; discard stems and gills. Brush mushroom caps with combined oil and garlic. Combine cheese, prosciutto and basil in medium bowl. Grill mushrooms, top side up, on covered grill over medium KINGSFORD® Briquets 4 minutes. Turn mushrooms over; fill caps with cheese mixture, dividing equally. Cover and grill 3 to 4 minutes longer until cheese mixture is warm. Remove mushrooms from grill; cut into quarters. Serve on mixed greens.   *Makes 4 servings*

Tomato, Potato and Basil Skillet

21

CHILIES

30-Minute Chili Mac

> 1 (1-pound) beef top round steak, cut into ¼-inch-thick strips
> ½ cup chopped onion
> 1 tablespoon vegetable oil
> 1 (16-ounce) can whole tomatoes, undrained, coarsely chopped
> ½ cup A.1.® Original or A.1.® Bold & Spicy Steak Sauce
> 2 tablespoons chili powder
> 1 cup uncooked elbow macaroni, cooked, drained
> 1 cup drained canned kidney beans, optional
> ⅓ cup shredded Cheddar cheese (about 1½ ounces)
> ¼ cup chopped fresh cilantro

In large skillet, over medium heat, cook steak and onion in oil 8 to 10 minutes, stirring occasionally. Stir in tomatoes with liquid, steak sauce and chili powder. Heat to a boil; reduce heat. Cover; simmer 10 minutes or until steak is tender. Stir in macaroni and beans, if desired. Sprinkle with cheese and cilantro. Serve immediately.   *Makes 4 servings*

Hot & Spicy Glazed Carrots

> 2 tablespoons vegetable oil
> 2 dried red chili peppers
> 1 pound carrots, peeled and cut diagonally into ⅛-inch slices
> ¼ cup KIKKOMAN® Teriyaki Baste & Glaze

Heat oil in hot wok or large skillet over high heat. Add peppers and stir-fry until darkened; remove and discard. Add carrots; reduce heat to medium. Stir-fry 4 minutes or until tender-crisp. Stir in teriyaki baste & glaze and cook until carrots are glazed. Serve immediately.   *Makes 4 servings*

30-Minute Chili Mac

Turkey Cutlets with Chipotle Pepper Mole

1 package BUTTERBALL® Fresh Boneless Turkey Breast Cutlets
1 can (14½ ounces) chicken broth
¼ cup raisins
4 cloves garlic, minced
1 chipotle chile pepper in adobo sauce
2 tablespoons ground almonds
2 teaspoons unsweetened cocoa
½ cup chopped fresh cilantro
2 tablespoons fresh lime juice
½ teaspoon salt

To prepare chipotle sauce, combine chicken broth, raisins, garlic, chile pepper, almonds and cocoa in medium saucepan. Simmer over low heat 10 minutes. Pour into food processor or blender; process until smooth. Add cilantro, lime juice and salt. Grill cutlets according to package directions. Serve chipotle sauce over grilled cutlets with Mexican polenta.* *Makes 7 servings*

To make Mexican polenta, cook 1 cup instant cornmeal polenta according to package directions. Stir in ½ teaspoon garlic powder, ½ teaspoon salt and 2 cups taco-seasoned cheese.

Prep Time: 20 minutes

Buffalo Chili Onions

½ cup FRANK'S® REDHOT® Hot Sauce
½ cup (1 stick) butter or margarine, melted or olive oil
¼ cup chili sauce
1 tablespoon chili powder
4 large sweet onions, cut into ½-inch-thick slices

Whisk together REDHOT sauce, butter, chili sauce and chili powder in medium bowl until blended; brush on onion slices.

Place onions on grid. Grill over medium-high coals 10 minutes or until tender, turning and basting often with the chili mixture. Serve warm.

Makes 6 side-dish servings

Tip: Onions may be prepared ahead and grilled just before serving.

Prep Time: 10 minutes
Cook Time: 10 minutes

Thai Chicken Curry

> 1 can (14½ ounces) **DEL MONTE**® **Original Recipe Stewed Tomatoes**
> 2 teaspoons curry powder
> 1 teaspoon sugar
> ½ teaspoon grated lemon peel
> ¼ to ½ teaspoon minced jalapeño chili
> 1 pound boneless, skinless chicken, cut into ¾-inch cubes
> ¾ cup coconut milk*
> 3 tablespoons thinly sliced fresh basil leaves *or* 1 teaspoon dried basil
> Hot cooked rice

If coconut milk is not available, omit sugar. Add 3 tablespoons shredded coconut to tomatoes. Substitute ½ cup whipping cream for coconut milk; add after chicken is done. Cook, uncovered, over low heat until heated through.

1. Combine tomatoes, curry, sugar, lemon peel and jalapeño in large skillet. Cook, uncovered, over medium-high heat 7 minutes or until thickened, stirring occasionally. Season chicken with salt and pepper, if desired.

2. Add chicken, coconut milk and basil to skillet.

3. Cover and cook over medium heat 8 minutes or until chicken is no longer pink. Serve over hot cooked rice.   *Makes 3 to 4 servings*

Prep and Cook Time: 25 minutes

Hot and Spicy Fruit Salad

> ⅓ cup orange juice
> 3 tablespoons lime juice
> 3 tablespoons minced fresh mint, basil or cilantro (optional)
> 2 jalapeño peppers, seeded, minced
> 1 tablespoon honey
> ½ small honeydew melon, cut into cubes
> 1 ripe large papaya, peeled, seeded, cubed
> 1 pint strawberries, stemmed, halved
> 1 can (8 ounces) pineapple chunks, drained

Blend orange juice, lime juice, mint, jalapeños and honey in small bowl. Combine melon, papaya, strawberries and pineapple in large bowl. Pour orange juice mixture over fruit; toss gently until well blended. Serve immediately, or cover and refrigerate up to 3 hours. Garnish with fresh mint, if desired.

Makes 6 servings

tasty tidbit

Chili powders, ground red (cayenne) pepper and red pepper flakes are all made from dried chilies. Whether you're working with fresh, dried or ground chilies, it is important to know that the longer you cook chilies, the hotter the dish will be. That's why a long-simmered stew with chilies may be quite hot, while a quick stir-fry with chilies has more flavor and less heat.

CHILIES

Hunan Chili Beef

1 pound beef flank steak
3 tablespoons reduced-sodium soy sauce
3 tablespoons vegetable oil, divided
1 tablespoon rice wine or dry sherry
1 tablespoon cornstarch
2 teaspoons brown sugar
1 cup drained canned baby corn
3 green onions, cut into 1-inch pieces
1 small piece fresh ginger (1 inch long), peeled and minced
2 cloves garlic, minced
¼ small red bell pepper, cut into ¼-inch strips
1 jalapeño pepper, halved, stemmed, seeded and cut into strips
1 teaspoon hot chili oil
Hot cooked rice

Cut beef across grain into 2×¼-inch slices. Combine soy sauce, 1 tablespoon vegetable oil, wine, cornstarch and brown sugar. Add beef and toss to coat. Heat wok over high heat 1 minute. Add 1 tablespoon vegetable oil and heat 30 seconds. Add half of beef mixture; stir-fry until well browned. Remove to large bowl. Repeat with remaining 1 tablespoon vegetable oil and beef mixture. Reduce heat to medium. Add corn, onions, ginger and garlic to wok; stir-fry 1 minute. Add red pepper and jalapeño; stir-fry 1 minute. Return beef to wok with chili oil; cook until heated through. Serve with rice.   *Makes 4 servings*

Grilled Fish with Roasted Jalapeño Rub

3 tablespoons chopped cilantro
2 tablespoons lime juice
1 tablespoon minced garlic
1 tablespoon minced fresh ginger
1 tablespoon minced roasted jalapeño peppers*
1½ pounds firm white fish fillets, such as orange roughy or red snapper
Lime wedges

*To roast peppers, place them on uncovered grill over hot coals. Grill until blistered, turning frequently. Remove from grill and place in large resealable plastic food storage bag for 15 minutes. Remove skins. Seed peppers, if desired, and cut into thin slices.

Combine cilantro, lime juice, garlic, ginger and peppers in small bowl. Lightly oil grid to prevent sticking. Grill fish on covered grill over hot KINGSFORD® Briquets 5 minutes. Turn; spread cilantro mixture on fish. Grill 3 to 5 minutes longer or until fish flakes easily when tested with fork. Serve with lime wedges.

Makes 4 servings

Hunan Chili Beef

CHILIES

Border Black Bean Chicken Salad

¼ cup olive oil, divided
1½ pounds boneless skinless chicken breasts, cut into 2-inch strips
1 clove garlic, minced
½ jalapeño pepper, seeded and finely chopped
1¼ teaspoons salt, divided
4 cups torn romaine lettuce
1 can (15 to 16 ounces) black beans, drained and rinsed
1 cup peeled and seeded cucumber cubes
1 cup red bell pepper strips
1 cup chopped tomato
½ cup chopped red onion
⅓ cup tomato vegetable juice
2 tablespoons fresh lime juice
½ teaspoon ground cumin
½ cup chopped pecans, toasted
Fresh parsley, for garnish

Heat 2 tablespoons oil in large skillet over medium heat until hot. Add chicken; stir-fry 2 minutes or until no longer pink in center. Add garlic, jalapeño and ¾ teaspoon salt; stir-fry 30 seconds. Combine chicken mixture, lettuce, beans, cucumber, red pepper, tomato and onion in large salad bowl. Combine tomato juice, lime juice, remaining 2 tablespoons oil, cumin and remaining ½ teaspoon salt in small jar with lid; shake well. Add to skillet; heat over medium heat until slightly warm. Pour warm dressing over chicken mixture; toss to coat. Sprinkle with pecans. Garnish with parsley. Serve immediately. *Makes 4 servings*

Favorite recipe from **National Chicken Council**

Tex-Mex Chunky Salsa Salad

3 to 4 medium tomatoes, halved, seeded and cubed (3 cups)
1 large (14 to 16 ounces) Texas SpringSweet® or Texas 1015® SuperSweet Onion, coarsely chopped
2 cucumbers, peeled, halved lengthwise, seeded and cubed
4 jalapeño or other small hot chili peppers, seeded and finely chopped (optional)
¼ cup fresh lemon juice
4 teaspoons minced garlic
1 tablespoon sugar

In medium bowl, combine all ingredients. Chill until ready to serve. If possible, make ahead so flavors can blend. *Makes 8 servings (about 2 quarts)*

Favorite recipe from **South Texas Onion Committee**

Border Black Bean Chicken Salad

CHILIES

spice note

To reduce the heat from chilies in your recipes, remove the seeds and the ribs from the chilies before cooking; they are the source of a chili pepper's heat.

Savory Corn Cakes

 2 cups all-purpose flour
 1 teaspoon baking powder
 ½ teaspoon salt
 2 cups frozen corn, thawed
 1 cup skim milk
 1 cup (4 ounces) shredded smoked Cheddar cheese
 2 egg whites, beaten
 1 whole egg, beaten
 4 green onions, finely chopped
 2 cloves garlic, minced
 1 tablespoon chili powder
 Prepared salsa (optional)

1. Combine flour, baking powder and salt in large bowl with wire whisk. Stir in corn, milk, cheese, egg whites, egg, green onions, garlic and chili powder until well blended.

2. Spray large nonstick skillet with nonstick cooking spray; heat over medium-high heat.

3. Drop batter by ¼ cupfuls into skillet. Cook 3 minutes per side or until golden brown. Serve with prepared salsa. *Makes 12 cakes*

South-of-the-Border Pizza

 1 prepared pizza shell or crust (about 12 inches)
 1 cup cooked kidney beans, rinsed and drained
 1 cup frozen corn, thawed
 1 tomato, chopped
 ¼ cup finely chopped fresh cilantro
 1 jalapeño pepper, finely chopped
 ¼ cup (4 ounces) shredded reduced-fat Monterey Jack cheese

1. Preheat oven to 450°F. Place pizza shell on ungreased pizza pan or baking sheet.

2. Arrange beans, corn, tomato, cilantro and jalapeño over pizza shell. Sprinkle evenly with cheese.

3. Bake pizza 8 to 10 minutes or until cheese is melted and lightly browned. Garnish with green bell pepper, if desired. *Makes 4 servings*

Savory Corn Cakes

CILANTRO

Broiled Caribbean Sea Bass

**6 skinless sea bass or striped bass fillets (5 to 6 ounces each),
   about ½ inch thick**
⅓ cup chopped cilantro
2 tablespoons olive oil
2 tablespoons fresh lime juice
2 teaspoons hot pepper sauce
2 cloves garlic, minced
1 package (7 ounces) black bean and rice mix
Lime wedges

1. Place fish in shallow dish. Combine cilantro, oil, lime juice, pepper sauce and garlic in small bowl; pour over fish. Cover; marinate in refrigerator 30 minutes or up to 2 hours.

2. Prepare black bean and rice mix according to package directions; keep warm.

3. Preheat broiler. Remove fish from marinade. Place fish on rack of broiler pan; drizzle with any remaining marinade in dish. Broil, 4 to 5 inches from heat, 8 to 10 minutes or until fish is opaque. Serve with black beans and rice and lime wedges. *Makes 6 servings*

Broiled Caribbean Sea Bass

CILANTRO

Turkey Burgers with Cilantro Pesto

1 pound ground turkey
½ cup chopped onion
¼ cup chunky salsa
1 jalapeño pepper, seeded and minced
1 teaspoon chopped garlic
½ teaspoon *each* dried oregano leaves and salt
4 hamburger buns, split and toasted
   Cilantro Pesto (recipe follows)

1. Prepare charcoal grill for direct-heat cooking.

2. In medium bowl combine turkey, onion, salsa, jalapeño, garlic, oregano and salt. Shape mixture into four burgers, approximately 4½ inches in diameter.

3. Grill 5 to 6 minutes per side until meat thermometer registers 160 to 165°F and meat is no longer pink in center.

4. To serve, place cooked burgers on bottom halves of buns; top each burger with 2 tablespoons Cilantro Pesto and top halves of buns.

Makes 4 servings

Cilantro Pesto

1 large clove garlic
1 cup packed cilantro leaves
¼ cup *each* chopped walnuts and Parmesan cheese
¼ teaspoon salt
¼ cup olive oil

1. In food processor, fitted with metal blade with motor running, drop garlic through feed tube to finely chop. Add cilantro, walnuts, cheese and salt. Process 45 seconds or until smooth. Scrape sides of bowl.

2. With motor running, slowly add olive oil and process until well blended. Cover and refrigerate several hours.

Makes ⅔ cup

Favorite recipe from **National Turkey Federation**

spice note

Coriander is the name of the plant whose leaves are most often called cilantro. All parts of the coriander plant are used and each has its own distinct flavor. The leaves are widely used in Mexican cooking, while the seeds are favored in Northern Europe, frequently used to flavor gin or as an ingredient in pickling spices. The root is used often in Thai curries and other Southeast Asian dishes.

Turkey Burger with Cilantro Pesto

CINNAMON

Cinnamon Bubble Ring

¼ **cup sugar**
½ **teaspoon ground cinnamon**
 1 **can (11 ounces each) refrigerated French bread dough**
1½ **tablespoons margarine or butter, melted**

1. Preheat oven to 350°F. Grease 9-inch tube pan. Combine sugar and cinnamon in small bowl.

2. Cut dough into 16 slices; roll into balls. Arrange 12 balls evenly spaced against outer wall of pan. Arrange remaining 4 balls evenly spaced against tube of pan. Brush with margarine. Sprinkle sugar mixture evenly over balls.

3. Bake 20 to 25 minutes or until golden brown. Serve warm.

Makes 8 servings

Tip: For a fast start to your morning, prepare the cinnamon buns in the pan, cover and refrigerate overnight. All you have to do in the morning is bake them for a quick, delicious treat.

Prep and Cook Time: 30 minutes

Cinnamon Bubble Ring

45

CINNAMON

Cinnamon is most frequently used for baking, but it is also commonly found in savory dishes of the Middle East. Cinnamon blends well with dried fruit for use in stuffings and cereals; it also adds flavor to curries, rice dishes and vegetables such as squash and sweet potatoes.

Persian Chicken Breasts

  1 **medium lemon**
  2 **teaspoons olive oil**
  1 **teaspoon ground cinnamon**
  ½ **teaspoon salt**
  ¼ **teaspoon ground black pepper**
  ¼ **teaspoon turmeric**
  4 **boneless skinless chicken breast halves**
  4 **flour tortillas or soft lavash (optional)**

1. Peel lemon rind into long strips with paring knife; reserve for garnish, if desired. Juice lemon; combine juice with oil, cinnamon, salt, pepper and turmeric in large heavy-duty resealable plastic food storage bag. Gently knead ingredients in bag to mix thoroughly; add chicken. Seal bag and turn to coat thoroughly. Refrigerate 4 hours or overnight.

2. Remove chicken from marinade and gently shake to remove excess. Grill chicken 5 to 7 minutes per side or until chicken is no longer pink in center, brushing occasionally with marinade. Discard remaining marinade. Serve chicken with lightly grilled tortillas or lavash and grilled vegetables, if desired.

Makes 4 servings

Cinnamon Honey Buns

  ¼ **cup butter or margarine, softened and divided**
  ½ **cup honey, divided**
  ¼ **cup chopped toasted nuts**
  2 **teaspoons ground cinnamon**
  1 **loaf (1 pound) frozen bread dough, thawed according to package directions**
  ⅔ **cup raisins**

Grease 12 muffin cups with 1 tablespoon butter. To prepare honey-nut topping, mix together 1 tablespoon butter, ¼ cup honey and chopped nuts. Place 1 teaspoon topping in each muffin cup. To prepare filling, mix together remaining 2 tablespoons butter, remaining ¼ cup honey and cinnamon. Roll out bread dough onto floured surface into 18×8-inch rectangle. Spread filling evenly over dough. Sprinkle with raisins. Starting with long side, roll dough into log. Cut log into 12 (1½-inch) slices. Place 1 slice, cut-side up, into each prepared muffin cup. Set muffin pan in warm place; let dough rise 30 minutes. Place muffin pan on foil-lined baking sheet. Bake at 375°F 20 minutes or until buns are golden brown. Remove from oven; cool in pan 5 minutes. Invert muffin pan to remove buns.

Makes 12 buns

Favorite recipe from **National Honey Board**

Persian Chicken Breast

CINNAMON

Cinnamon Stars

2 tablespoons sugar
¾ teaspoon ground cinnamon
¾ cup butter or margarine, softened
2 egg yolks
1 teaspoon vanilla extract
1 package DUNCAN HINES® Moist Deluxe French Vanilla Cake Mix

1. Preheat oven to 375°F. Combine sugar and cinnamon in small bowl. Set aside.

2. Combine butter, egg yolks and vanilla extract in large bowl. Blend in cake mix gradually. Roll to ⅛-inch thickness on lightly floured surface. Cut with 2½-inch star cookie cutter. Place 2 inches apart on ungreased baking sheet.

3. Sprinkle cookies with cinnamon-sugar mixture. Bake at 375°F for 6 to 8 minutes or until edges are light golden brown. Cool 1 minute on baking sheet. Remove to cooling rack. Cool completely. Store in airtight container.

Makes 3 to 3½ dozen cookies

Tip: *You can use your favorite cookie cutter in place of the star cookie cutter.*

Apple-Cranberry Crisp

1½ cups QUAKER® Oats (quick or old fashioned, uncooked)
½ cup firmly packed brown sugar
⅓ cup all-purpose flour
½ teaspoon ground cinnamon
⅓ cup vegetable shortening, melted
1 tablespoon water
1 can (16 ounces) whole berry cranberry sauce
2 tablespoons cornstarch
5 cups peeled and thinly sliced apples (about 5 medium)

Preheat oven to 375°F. For topping, combine oats, brown sugar, flour and cinnamon; mix well. Stir in melted shortening and water; mix until crumbly. Set aside.

For filling, combine cranberry sauce and cornstarch in large saucepan; mix well. Heat over medium-heat, stirring occasionally, 2 minutes or until sauce bubbles. Add apples, tossing to coat. Spread into 8-inch baking dish. Crumble topping over fruit. Bake 25 to 35 minutes or until apples are tender. Serve warm with whipped cream or ice cream, if desired.

Makes 9 servings

Cinnamon Stars

CUMIN

Texas-Style Short Ribs

2 tablespoons chili powder
1 tablespoon LAWRY'S® Seasoned Salt
2 teaspoons LAWRY'S® Garlic Powder with Parsley
2 teaspoons ground cumin
1 teaspoon ground coriander
¼ teaspoon hot pepper sauce (optional)
5 pounds trimmed beef short ribs
1 bottle (12 ounces) chili sauce
1 cup finely chopped onion
1 cup dry red wine
½ cup water
½ cup beef broth
½ cup olive oil

In small bowl, combine chili powder, Seasoned Salt, Garlic Powder with Parsley, cumin, coriander and hot pepper sauce, if desired; mix well. Rub both sides of ribs with spice mixture. Place in large resealable plastic food storage bag; refrigerate 1 hour. In medium bowl, combine remaining ingredients. Remove ½ cup marinade for basting. Add additional marinade to ribs; seal bag. Marinate in refrigerator at least 1 hour. Remove ribs; discard used marinade. Grill ribs over low heat 45 to 60 minutes or until tender, turning once and basting often with additional ½ cup marinade. *Do not baste during last 5 minutes of cooking.* Discard any remaining marinade.

Makes 8 to 10 servings

Serving Suggestion: *Serve with coleslaw and potato wedges.*

Hint: *Ribs may be baked in 375°F. oven 45 to 60 minutes or until tender, turning once and basting often with additional ½ cup marinade.*

Texas-Style Short Ribs

GARLIC

Roasted Pepper Focaccia

- **1 medium green bell pepper**
- **1 medium yellow bell pepper**
- **2 tablespoons yellow cornmeal**
- **2 tablespoons olive oil, divided**
- **1 cup thin yellow onion rings**
- **1 tablespoon minced garlic**
- **1 pound frozen bread dough, thawed**
- **1 teaspoon freshly ground black pepper**
- **2 teaspoons finely chopped fresh rosemary leaves**
- **1 cup (4 ounces) shredded ALPINE LACE® Reduced Fat Mozzarella Cheese**

1. Preheat the broiler. Place the bell peppers on a baking sheet. Broil 3 inches from heat for 7 minutes or until blackened, turning frequently. Transfer to a paper bag, close tightly and let stand 15 minutes or until peppers are soft. Scrape off outside skins; seed and cut the peppers into thin strips. (You will have about 1½ cups.)

2. Preheat the oven to 425°F. Spray a 15-inch pizza pan with nonstick cooking spray and sprinkle with the cornmeal. Spray a medium-size skillet with the cooking spray.

3. In the skillet, heat 1 tablespoon of the oil over medium-high heat. Add the onion and garlic and sauté for 5 minutes; keep warm.

4. Gently press the bread dough onto the bottom and up the sides of the pan. Brush the dough with the remaining tablespoon of oil; sprinkle with the black pepper. Using your fingertips, dimple the dough all over, pressing in the pepper at the same time. Sprinkle with the rosemary.

5. Top the dough with the onion mixture and the bell peppers. Sprinkle with the mozzarella. Bake, uncovered, for 12 to 15 minutes or until the cheese melts and the focaccia is golden brown. *Makes 8 servings*

Roasted Pepper Focaccia

GARLIC

BBQ Pork Stir Fry

1 (2-cup) bag **UNCLE BEN'S®** Boil-in-Bag Rice
1 pound whole pork tenderloin
1 tablespoon oil
2 teaspoons minced garlic
2 teaspoons minced fresh ginger
1 package (16 ounces) frozen stir-fry vegetable medley
⅔ cup barbecue sauce
2 tablespoons chopped cilantro (optional)

1. Cook rice according to package directions.

2. Trim tenderloin of any fat; cut in half lengthwise, then into ¼-inch slices.

3. Heat oil in large skillet over medium-high heat until hot. Add pork, garlic and ginger; cook about 3 minutes or until pork is no longer pink.

4. Add vegetables and ¼ cup water. Cover; cook 3 minutes, stirring occasionally.

5. Stir in barbecue sauce. Cover; reduce heat and simmer 5 to 7 minutes or just until vegetables are tender and pork is cooked through.

6. Serve pork and vegetables over rice. Garnish with chopped cilantro, if desired.   *Makes 4 servings*

Cook's Tip: *Choose a stir-fry vegetable medley, such as sugar snap peas, carrots, onions and mushrooms for this recipe.*

Garlicky Green Beans

5 large cloves garlic, peeled
¼ cup vegetable oil
2 packages (9 ounces each) frozen cut green beans, thawed and drained
⅓ cup **KIKKOMAN®** Stir-Fry Sauce

Thinly slice 4 garlic cloves. Heat oil in wok or small saucepan over medium heat until hot. Add thinly sliced garlic; cook about 2 minutes, or until lightly browned, stirring occasionally. Remove with slotted spoon and drain on paper towels. Mince remaining garlic clove. Remove and reserve 1 tablespoon garlic oil. (Pour remaining garlic oil in container. Cover and refrigerate; use within a few days.) Return reserved oil to same pan; heat over medium-high heat. Add green beans and minced garlic; stir-fry 5 minutes. Reduce heat to low; pour in stir-fry sauce. Cook, stirring, until beans are coated with sauce. Just before serving, sprinkle garlic chips over beans.   *Makes 6 servings*

BBQ Pork Stir Fry

69

Spicy-Sweet Brisket

4 to 5 pounds boneless beef brisket, well trimmed
1 pound fresh mushrooms, cleaned but not sliced
3 carrots, cut into 2-inch pieces
3 onions, thinly sliced
1 rib celery, cut into 2-inch pieces
1 (26-ounce) jar NEWMAN'S OWN® Diavolo Sauce
½ cup water
½ cup packed brown sugar
1 tablespoon garlic powder
½ teaspoon black pepper

Preheat oven to 350°F. Brown meat in large ungreased skillet. Remove to large Dutch oven. Add vegetables to meat. In separate bowl, combine Diavolo Sauce, water and brown sugar; stir and pour over meat. Sprinkle with garlic powder and pepper.

Cover tightly and bake 3 hours. Remove cover and allow meat to slightly brown 30 minutes.

Brisket should be made a day ahead of time and refrigerated overnight to allow flavors to blend. Thinly slice brisket across the grain.

Makes 12 servings

Vegetables in Garlic Cream Sauce

1 cup water
4 cups cut-up vegetables such as DOLE® Asparagus, Bell Peppers, Broccoli, Carrots, Cauliflower or Sugar Peas
1 teaspoon olive or vegetable oil
4 cloves garlic, finely chopped
⅓ cup fat free or reduced fat mayonnaise
⅓ cup nonfat or low fat milk
2 tablespoons chopped fresh parsley

• Place water in large saucepan; bring to a boil. Add vegetables; reduce heat to low. Cook, uncovered, 9 to 12 minutes or until vegetables are tender-crisp; meanwhile, prepare sauce.

• Heat oil in small saucepan over medium heat. Add garlic; cook and stir garlic until golden brown. Remove from heat; stir in mayonnaise and milk.

• Drain vegetables; place in serving bowl. Pour in garlic sauce; toss to evenly coat. Sprinkle with parsley.

Makes 4 servings

Prep Time: 10 minutes
Cook Time: 15 minutes

Arroz con Pollo

1 (3-pound) broiler-fryer chicken, cut up
½ teaspoon ground cumin
1 tablespoon vegetable oil
1 can (14½ ounces) **DEL MONTE®** Mexican Recipe Stewed Tomatoes
1 cup uncooked long grain white rice
1 can (14 ounces) chicken broth
1 large onion, thinly sliced
2 cloves garlic, minced
1 to 1½ teaspoons minced jalapeño chile

1. Sprinkle chicken with cumin. Season with salt and pepper, if desired.

2. Brown chicken in oil in 4-quart heavy saucepan over medium-high heat; drain. Drain tomatoes reserving ⅓ cup liquid.

3. Add reserved liquid, tomatoes and remaining ingredients to saucepan.

4. Cover and cook over low heat about 30 minutes or until chicken is no longer pink and rice is tender.   *Makes 6 servings*

Prep and Cook Time: 45 minutes

Penne with Arrabiatta Sauce

½ pound uncooked penne or other tube-shaped pasta
2 tablespoons olive oil or oil from sun-dried tomatoes
8 cloves garlic
1 can (28 ounces) crushed tomatoes in purée
¼ cup chopped sun-dried tomatoes packed in oil
3 tablespoons **FRANK'S® REDHOT®** Hot Sauce
8 kalamata olives, pitted and chopped*
6 fresh basil leaves or 1½ teaspoons dried basil leaves
1 tablespoon capers

To pit olives, place on cutting board. Press with side of knife until olives split. Remove pits.

1. Cook pasta according to package directions; drain.

2. Heat oil in large nonstick skillet over medium heat. Add garlic; cook until golden, stirring frequently. Add remaining ingredients. Bring to a boil. Simmer, partially covered, 10 minutes. Stir occasionally.

3. Toss pasta with half of the sauce mixture. Spoon into serving bowl. Pour remaining sauce mixture over pasta. Garnish with fresh basil or parsley, if desired.   *Makes 4 servings (3 cups sauce)*

Prep Time: 15 minutes
Cook Time: 20 minutes

tasty tidbit

Because mincing or pressing garlic releases more of its essential oils, it is much stronger than sliced or whole garlic. To add a mild garlic flavor to a dish, rub a crushed clove around the inside of a wooden salad bowl, skillet, baking dish or fondue pot.

GARLIC

Potatoes and Leeks au Gratin

5 tablespoons butter or margarine, divided
2 large leeks
2 tablespoons minced garlic
2 pounds baking potatoes, peeled (about 4 medium)
1 cup heavy cream
1 cup milk
3 eggs
2 teaspoons salt
¼ teaspoon white pepper
2 to 3 slices dense, day-old white bread, such as French or Italian
2 ounces Parmesan cheese
Fresh chives and salad burnet for garnish

1. Preheat oven to 375°F. Generously butter shallow oval 10-cup baking dish with 1 tablespoon butter; set aside.

2. To prepare leeks, cut leeks lengthwise in half; wash thoroughly. Cut leeks crosswise into ¼-inch slices.

3. Melt 2 tablespoons butter in large skillet over medium heat. Add leeks and garlic. Cook and stir 8 to 10 minutes until leeks are softened. Remove from heat; set aside.

4. Cut potatoes crosswise into ¹⁄₁₆-inch-thick slices. Layer half of potato slices in prepared baking dish. Top with half of leek mixture. Repeat layers once with remaining potato slices and leek mixture. Whisk together cream, milk, eggs, salt and pepper in medium bowl until well blended; pour evenly over leek mixture.

5. To prepare bread crumbs, tear bread slices into 1-inch pieces and place in food processor or blender; process until fine crumbs form. Measure ¾ cup crumbs. Grate cheese into small bowl; stir in bread crumbs. Melt remaining 2 tablespoons butter in small saucepan; pour over crumbs, tossing to blend thoroughly. Sprinkle crumb mixture evenly over cream mixture.

6. Bake 50 to 60 minutes until top is golden and potatoes in center are tender when pierced with tip of sharp knife. Remove from oven; let stand 5 to 10 minutes before serving. Garnish, if desired. *Makes 6 to 8 servings*

Potatoes and Leeks au Gratin

GARLIC

The most common variety of garlic is American garlic, which has white skin and a strong flavor. The pink-skinned Mexican and Italian garlic taste sweeter, and elephant garlic, with its large cloves, is very mild.

Skillet Chicken Vesuvio

1	package (6.9 ounces) RICE-A-RONI® Chicken Flavor
12	unpeeled garlic cloves
3	tablespoons olive oil or vegetable oil
1½	teaspoons dried oregano leaves
½	teaspoon salt (optional)
½	teaspoon freshly ground black pepper
¼	teaspoon dried rosemary (optional)
4	skinless, boneless chicken breast halves
1	medium tomato, chopped
4	lemon wedges (optional)

1. Prepare Rice-A-Roni® Mix as package directs.

2. While Rice-A-Roni® is simmering, combine garlic cloves and oil in second large skillet. Cover; cook over medium heat 5 minutes.

3. Combine seasonings; sprinkle over chicken.

4. Push garlic to edge of skillet. Add chicken; cook about 5 minutes on each side or until chicken is no longer pink inside. Remove garlic with slotted spoon. Squeeze softened garlic over chicken; discard garlic peels.

5. Stir tomato into rice. Serve rice topped with chicken, juices and lemon wedges.

Makes 4 servings

Peppered Pecans

3	tablespoons butter or margarine
3	cloves garlic, minced
1½	teaspoons TABASCO® brand Pepper Sauce
½	teaspoon salt
3	cups pecan halves

Preheat oven to 250°F. Melt butter in small skillet. Add garlic, TABASCO® Sauce and salt; cook 1 minute. Toss pecans with butter mixture; spread in single layer on baking sheet. Bake 1 hour or until pecans are crisp, stirring occasionally.

Makes 3 cups

Skillet Chicken Vesuvio

GINGER

Sweet & Sour Cashew Chicken

    1 **can (16 ounces) cling peach slices in syrup**
    1 **cup KIKKOMAN® Sweet & Sour Sauce**
    2 **boneless, skinless chicken breast halves**
    1 **tablespoon cornstarch**
    1 **tablespoon KIKKOMAN® Soy Sauce**
    1 **tablespoon minced fresh ginger root**
  ½ **teaspoon sugar**
    2 **tablespoons vegetable oil, divided**
    1 **onion, chunked**
    1 **green bell pepper, chunked**
    1 **small carrot, cut diagonally into thin slices**
  ⅓ **cup roasted cashews**

Reserving ⅓ cup syrup, drain peaches; cut slices in half. Blend reserved syrup and sweet & sour sauce; set aside. Cut chicken into 1-inch-square pieces. Combine cornstarch, soy sauce, ginger and sugar in medium bowl; stir in chicken. Heat 1 tablespoon oil in hot wok or large skillet over high heat. Add chicken and stir-fry 4 minutes; remove. Heat remaining 1 tablespoon oil in same pan. Add onion, bell pepper and carrot; stir-fry 4 minutes. Stir in chicken, sweet & sour sauce mixture, peaches and cashews; heat through. Serve immediately.

Makes 4 servings

Sweet & Sour Cashew Chicken

GINGER

Store unpeeled fresh ginger root in the refrigerator sealed in a plastic food storage bag for up to 3 weeks.

Ginger Baked Bananas with Cinnamon Cream

  4 firm ripe bananas, peeled
 ¼ cup butter or margarine, melted and divided
  1 tablespoon lemon juice
 ¼ cup packed brown sugar
 ¼ cup quick or old-fashioned oats
 ¼ cup chopped pecans or walnuts
  1 tablespoon finely chopped crystallized ginger
  1 teaspoon granulated sugar
 ½ teaspoon ground cinnamon
 ½ cup chilled whipping cream

1. Preheat oven to 375°F. Place bananas in baking dish large enough to hold them in single layer.

2. Combine 2 tablespoons butter and lemon juice in small bowl; drizzle evenly over bananas.

3. Combine brown sugar, oats, pecans, ginger and remaining 2 tablespoons butter; sprinkle evenly over bananas. Bake 15 to 18 minutes or until bananas are hot and topping is bubbly.

4. To prepare Cinnamon Cream, combine granulated sugar and cinnamon in cup. Chill large bowl and beaters thoroughly. Pour chilled whipping cream into chilled bowl and beat with electric mixer at high speed until soft peaks form. Gradually beat sugar mixture into whipped cream until stiff peaks form.

5. Serve bananas warm with Cinnamon Cream.   *Makes 4 servings*

Spicy Apple Chutney

  1 pound cooking apples
  1 cup chopped onion
  1 cup sugar
 ½ cup raisins
 ½ cup water
 ⅓ cup KIKKOMAN® Teriyaki Marinade & Sauce
 ¼ cup vinegar
  2 tablespoons minced fresh ginger root

Peel, core and coarsely chop apples. Combine apples with onion, sugar, raisins, water, teriyaki sauce, vinegar and ginger in Dutch oven or large saucepan; bring to boil over medium-high heat. Reduce heat to low; simmer, uncovered, 30 minutes, or until thickened, stirring occasionally. Place in covered container; refrigerate several days for flavors to blend.   *Makes 2 cups*

Ginger Baked Bananas with Cinnamon Cream

81

GINGER

tasty tidbit

Dried, ground ginger tastes very different from fresh, so the two types are not always interchangeable in recipes. Fresh ginger is used in meat, fish, vegetable dishes and sauces; ground ginger is frequently found in baked goods but also adds flavor to soups, curries and meat or poultry recipes.

Asian Pockets

　1　**pound BOB EVANS® Original Recipe Roll Sausage**
　¼　**cup chopped green onions**
　2　**teaspoons minced fresh ginger**
　¾　**teaspoon garlic powder**
　1　**tablespoon vegetable oil**
　1　**large green bell pepper, sliced lengthwise**
　1　**large red bell pepper, sliced lengthwise**
　6　**small white pita bread pockets**
　12　**tablespoons apple butter, divided**

Combine sausage, green onions, ginger and garlic powder in medium bowl; mix well. Shape mixture into 6 patties. Cook patties in medium skillet over medium heat until browned and cooked through. Set aside and keep warm. Add oil and bell peppers to same skillet; cook and stir 1 to 2 minutes over medium heat just until peppers are slightly tender.

Open each pita bread pocket; fill with sausage patty, 2 tablespoons pepper mixture and 2 tablespoons apple butter. Serve warm. Refrigerate leftovers.

Makes 6 servings

Peppery Gingerbread

　2　**cups all-purpose flour**
　1　**cup light molasses**
　¾　**cup milk**
　½　**cup sugar**
　½　**cup butter or margarine, softened**
　1　**tablespoon TABASCO® brand Pepper Sauce**
　1½　**teaspoons ground ginger**
　1　**teaspoon baking soda**
　1　**teaspoon ground cinnamon**
　1　**large egg**
　　Confectioners' sugar

Preheat oven to 325°F. Grease and flour 9-inch square baking pan. Beat flour, molasses, milk, sugar, butter, TABASCO® Sauce, ginger, baking soda, cinnamon and egg in large bowl with mixer at low speed until well blended and smooth. Increase speed to medium; beat 2 minutes, occasionally scraping bowl with rubber spatula.

Pour batter into prepared pan; bake 1 hour or until toothpick inserted in center comes out clean. Cool in pan on wire rack. Sprinkle top of gingerbread with confectioners' sugar.

Makes 12 servings

Asian Pocket

GINGER

Ginger Cream Banana Pie

1½ **cups gingersnap cookie crumbs**
¼ **cup margarine, softened**
2¼ **cups milk**
 1 **package (5.9 ounces) instant vanilla pudding (6 servings)**
 1 **tablespoon crystallized ginger**
 1 **tablespoon grated orange peel**
 4 **firm, medium DOLE® Bananas**

• Combine gingersnap crumbs and margarine in bowl. Press on bottom and up side of 9-inch pie plate. Bake at 350°F 5 minutes. Cool.

• Combine milk, pudding, ginger and orange peel until well blended. Slice 2 bananas into bottom of pie shell. Cover with one-half filling. Slice remaining bananas over filling. Top with remaining filling. Press plastic wrap on surface. Refrigerate 3 hours. Garnish with additional banana slices, orange curls and edible flowers, if desired.   *Makes 8 servings*

Prep Time: 25 minutes
Chill Time: 3 hours

Tomato Ginger Beef

 2 **tablespoons dry sherry**
 1 **tablespoon soy sauce**
 2 **cloves garlic, crushed**
 1 **teaspoon minced gingerroot or** ¼ **teaspoon ground ginger**
 1 **pound flank steak, thinly sliced**
 1 **tablespoon cornstarch**
 1 **tablespoon vegetable oil**
 1 **can (14½ ounces) DEL MONTE® Original Recipe Stewed Tomatoes**
  Hot cooked rice

1. Combine sherry, soy sauce, garlic and ginger; toss with meat. Stir in cornstarch; mix well.

2. Cook meat mixture in oil in large skillet over high heat until browned, stirring constantly.

3. Add tomatoes; cook over high heat until thickened, stirring frequently, about 5 minutes. Serve over hot cooked rice. Garnish with sliced green onions, if desired.   *Makes 4 to 6 servings*

Hint: Partially freeze meat for easier slicing.

Prep Time: 10 minutes
Cook Time: 12 minutes

Honey-Citrus Glazed Veal Chops

3 tablespoons fresh lime juice
2 tablespoons honey
2 teaspoons grated fresh ginger
½ teaspoon grated lime peel
4 veal rib chops, cut 1 inch thick (about 8 ounces each)

Stir together lime juice, honey, ginger and lime peel in small bowl. Place veal rib chops in glass dish just large enough to hold chops. Brush lime mixture liberally over both sides of chops. Refrigerate, covered, 30 minutes while preparing coals.* Remove chops from dish; brush with any remaining lime mixture. Place chops on grid over medium coals. Grill 12 to 14 minutes for medium (160°F) or to desired doneness, turning once. (Or, broil 4 to 5 inches from heat source 5 to 6 minutes per side for medium or to desired doneness, turning once.)

Makes 4 servings

To check temperature of coals, cautiously hold palm of hand about 4 inches above coals. Count the number of seconds you can hold it in that position before the heat forces you to pull it away (about 4 seconds for medium coals is normal).

Prep Time: 10 minutes
Cook Time: 12 to 14 minutes

Favorite recipe from **National Cattlemen's Beef Association**

spice note

For fresh grated ginger, first peel away the rough outer skin, then grate the flesh on a ginger grater (sold in many Asian markets) or other fine graters. For a quick fix, take a small, peeled chunk of ginger and use a garlic press to mince it.

Orange Ginger Chicken & Rice

1 package (6.9 ounces) RICE-A-RONI® With ⅓ Less Salt Chicken Flavor
1 tablespoon margarine or butter
1 cup orange juice
¾ pound skinless boneless chicken breasts, cut into thin strips
2 cloves garlic, minced
¼ teaspoon ground ginger
    Dash red pepper flakes (optional)
1½ cups carrots, cut into short thin strips or 3 cups broccoli flowerets

1. In large skillet, sauté Rice-A-Roni® mix and margarine over medium heat, stirring frequently until vermicelli is golden brown.

2. Stir in 1½ cups water, orange juice, chicken, garlic, ginger, red pepper flakes and contents of seasoning packet; bring to a boil over high heat.

3. Cover; reduce heat. Simmer 10 minutes.

4. Stir in carrots. Cover; continue to simmer 5 to 10 minutes or until liquid is absorbed and rice is tender.

Makes 4 servings

GINGER

Pumpkin-Ginger Scones

½ **cup sugar, divided**
2 **cups all-purpose flour**
2 **teaspoons baking powder**
1 **teaspoon ground cinnamon**
½ **teaspoon baking soda**
½ **teaspoon salt**
5 **tablespoons butter or margarine, divided**
1 **egg**
½ **cup solid pack pumpkin**
¼ **cup sour cream**
½ **teaspoon grated fresh ginger**

Preheat oven to 425°F. Reserve 1 tablespoon sugar. Combine remaining sugar, flour, baking powder, cinnamon, baking soda and salt in large bowl. Cut in 4 tablespoons butter with pastry blender until mixture resembles coarse crumbs. Beat egg in small bowl. Add pumpkin, sour cream and ginger; beat until well combined. Add to flour mixture; stir until mixture forms soft dough. Turn dough out onto well-floured surface. Knead 10 times. Roll dough into 9×6-inch rectangle. Cut dough into 6 (3-inch) squares. Cut each square diagonally in half, making 12 triangles. Place triangles, 2 inches apart, on ungreased baking sheets. Melt remaining 1 tablespoon butter. Brush with butter and sprinkle with reserved sugar. Bake 10 to 12 minutes or until golden brown. Cool 10 minutes on wire racks. Serve warm. *Makes 12 scones*

Chinese Spinach Toss

3 **to 4 cups fresh bean sprouts *or* 2 cans (16 ounces each) bean sprouts, well drained**
⅓ **cup honey**
⅓ **cup white wine or rice vinegar**
2 **tablespoons vegetable oil**
2 **teaspoons soy sauce**
1 **to 2 teaspoons grated fresh gingerroot**
6 **cups washed and torn fresh spinach**
1 **cup diced peeled jicama**
1 **cup crisp Chinese noodles**

Place bean sprouts in large glass or ceramic bowl. Combine honey, vinegar, oil, soy sauce and gingerroot in small bowl; pour over bean sprouts. Cover and refrigerate at least 1 hour, tossing occasionally. Just before serving, add spinach and jicama; toss to coat. Top with noodles. *Makes 6 servings*

Favorite recipe from **National Honey Board**

Pumpkin-Ginger Scones

NUTMEG

Apple and Brie Omelet

2 large Golden Delicious apples
2 tablespoons butter or margarine, divided
½ teaspoon ground nutmeg
4 ounces Brie cheese
8 large eggs, lightly beaten
2 green onions, thinly sliced

1. Place large serving platter in oven and preheat to 200°F. Peel, core and slice apples; place in microwavable container. Top with 1 tablespoon butter and nutmeg. Cover and microwave on HIGH (100% power) 3 minutes. Set aside. While apples cook, trim rind from cheese; thinly slice cheese.

2. Melt 1½ teaspoons butter in medium nonstick skillet over medium heat; rotate skillet to coat bottom. Place eggs in medium bowl and whisk until blended. Pour half of eggs into skillet. Let cook, without stirring, 1 to 2 minutes, or until set on bottom. With rubber spatula, lift sides of omelet and slightly tilt pan to allow uncooked portion of egg flow underneath. Cover pan and cook 2 to 3 minutes, until eggs are set but still moist on top. Remove platter from oven and slide omelet into center. Spread apples evenly over entire omelet, reserving a few slices for garnish, if desired. Evenly space cheese slices over apples. Sprinkle with onion, reserving some for garnish. Return platter to oven.

3. Cook remaining beaten eggs in remaining 1½ teaspoons butter as directed above. When cooked, slide spatula around edges to be certain omelet is loose. Carefully place second omelet over cheese, apple and onion mixture. Top with reserved apple and onion slices. Cut into wedges to serve.

Makes 4 servings

Apple and Brie Omelet

NUTMEG

Sweet Potato Ravioli with Asiago Cheese Sauce

¾ **pound sweet potato**
2 **tablespoons plain nonfat yogurt**
1 **teaspoon minced fresh chives**
1 **tablespoon plus ¼ teaspoon minced fresh sage, divided**
24 **wonton wrappers**
1 **tablespoon reduced-calorie margarine**
1 **tablespoon plus 2 teaspoons all-purpose flour**
½ **cup skim milk**
½ **cup fat-free reduced-sodium chicken broth**
½ **cup (2 ounces) shredded Asiago or Cheddar cheese**
¼ **teaspoon ground nutmeg**
¼ **teaspoon ground white pepper**
⅛ **teaspoon ground cinnamon**

1. Preheat oven to 350°F. Bake sweet potato 40 to 45 minutes or until tender. Cool completely. Peel potato and mash pulp. Stir in yogurt, chives and ¼ teaspoon sage.

2. Place wonton wrappers on counter. Spoon 1 rounded teaspoon potato mixture in center of each wonton. Spread filling flat leaving ½-inch border. Brush edges lightly with water. Fold wontons in half diagonally, pressing lightly to seal. Place filled wontons on baking sheet and cover loosely with plastic wrap.

3. Bring 1½ quarts water to a boil in large saucepan. Reduce heat to medium. Add a few ravioli at a time. (Do not overcrowd.) Cook until tender, about 9 minutes. Transfer to platter with slotted spoon.

4. Melt margarine in small saucepan. Stir in flour; cook 1 minute, stirring constantly. Gradually stir in milk and chicken broth. Cook and stir until slightly thickened, about 4 minutes. Stir in cheese, nutmeg, white pepper and cinnamon.

5. Spoon 3 tablespoons sauce onto individual plates. Place 3 ravioli onto each plate. Sprinkle with remaining sage. *Makes 8 servings*

Sweet Potato Ravioli with Asiago Cheese Sauce

NUTMEG

Pasta with Spinach-Cheese Sauce

¼ **cup FILIPPO BERIO® Extra-Virgin Olive Oil, divided**
1 **medium onion, chopped**
1 **clove garlic, chopped**
3 **cups chopped fresh spinach, washed and well drained**
1 **cup low-fat ricotta or cottage cheese**
½ **cup chopped fresh parsley**
1 **teaspoon dried basil leaves**
1 **teaspoon lemon juice**
¼ **teaspoon black pepper**
¼ **teaspoon ground nutmeg**
¾ **pound uncooked spaghetti**

1. Heat 3 tablespoons olive oil in large skillet over medium heat. Cook and stir onion and garlic until onion is tender.

2. Add spinach to skillet; cook 3 to 5 minutes or until spinach wilts.

3. Place spinach mixture, cheese, parsley, basil, lemon juice, pepper and nutmeg in covered blender container. Blend until smooth. Leave in blender, covered, to keep sauce warm.

4. Cook pasta according to package directions. Do not overcook. Drain pasta, reserving ¼ cup water. In large bowl, toss pasta with remaining 1 tablespoon olive oil.

5. Add reserved ¼ cup water to sauce in blender. Blend; serve over pasta.

Makes 4 servings

Stuffed French Toast

1 **(8-ounce) package cream cheese, softened**
2 **tablespoons sugar**
1½ **teaspoons vanilla, divided**
¼ **teaspoon ground cinnamon**
½ **cup chopped walnuts or pecans**
1 **(1-pound) loaf French bread**
4 **eggs**
1 **cup whipping cream or half and half**
½ **teaspoon nutmeg**
1 **cup (12-ounce jar) SMUCKER'S® Apricot Preserves**
½ **cup orange juice**
½ **teaspoon almond extract**
   Fresh fruit

Beat together cream cheese, sugar, 1 teaspoon vanilla and cinnamon until fluffy. Stir in nuts; set aside.

Cut bread into 10 to 12 (1½-inch) slices; cut pocket in top of each slice. Fill each pocket with about 1½ tablespoons cream cheese mixture.

Beat together eggs, whipping cream, remaining ½ teaspoon vanilla and nutmeg. Using tongs, dip bread slices in egg mixture, being careful not to squeeze out filling. Cook on a lightly greased griddle until both sides are golden brown. (To keep cooked slices hot for serving, place on baking sheet in warm oven.)

Meanwhile, combine and heat preserves and orange juice. Stir in almond extract. To serve, drizzle apricot mixture over French toast. Serve with fresh fruit.

Makes 10 to 12 slices

Nita Lou's Cream of Broccoli Soup

⅓ **cup plus 1 tablespoon WESSON® Vegetable Oil**
3 **cups coarsely chopped broccoli florets and stems**
1 **cup diced carrots**
1½ **cups fresh chopped leeks**
3 **tablespoons all-purpose flour**
1½ **teaspoons minced fresh garlic**
2 **(12-ounce) cans evaporated milk**
1½ **cups homemade chicken stock or canned chicken broth**
½ **teaspoon garlic salt**
¼ **teaspoon ground nutmeg**
⅛ **teaspoon pepper**
3 **tablespoons chopped fresh parsley**
Salt to taste

In a large saucepan, heat 3 tablespoons Wesson® Oil. Add broccoli and carrots; sauté until tender. Remove vegetables; set aside. Add remaining oil, leeks, flour and garlic; sauté until leeks are limp and flour is lightly browned, about 2 minutes, stirring constantly. Whisk in the evaporated milk and stock. Continue to cook, whisking constantly until the flour has dissolved and the mixture is smooth. *Do not bring mixture to a boil.* Reduce heat to LOW. Add cooked vegetables along with any juices, garlic salt, nutmeg and pepper. Simmer 5 minutes longer, being careful not to bring soup to a boil. Remove the pan from the heat; stir in parsley. Let soup stand 5 minutes before serving. Salt to taste. *Makes 6 servings*

tasty tidbit

Nutmeg is a versatile spice— it is commonly used in eggnog, puddings and fruit pies, but is also found in sausage and meat recipes, soups and sauces, and a variety of Italian pasta dishes.

Spicy Lemon Crescents

    1 cup (2 sticks) butter or margarine, softened
1½ cups powdered sugar, divided
  ½ teaspoon lemon extract
  ½ teaspoon grated lemon zest
    2 cups cake flour
  ½ cup finely chopped almonds, walnuts or pecans
    1 teaspoon ground cinnamon
  ½ teaspoon ground cardamom
  ½ teaspoon ground nutmeg
1¾ cups "M&M's"® Chocolate Mini Baking Bits

Preheat oven to 375°F. Lightly grease cookie sheets; set aside. In large bowl cream butter and ½ cup sugar; add lemon extract and zest until well blended. In medium bowl combine flour, nuts, cinnamon, cardamom and nutmeg; add to creamed mixture until well blended. Stir in "M&M's"® Chocolate Mini Baking Bits. Using 1 tablespoon of dough at a time, form into crescent shapes; place about 2 inches apart onto prepared cookie sheets. Bake 12 to 14 minutes or until edges are golden. Cool 2 minutes on cookie sheets. Gently roll warm crescents in remaining 1 cup sugar. Cool completely on wire racks. Store in tightly covered container.   ***Makes about 2 dozen cookies***

Honey-Glazed Sweet Potatoes

1½ pounds sweet potatoes or yams, peeled and quartered
  ⅔ cup orange juice, divided
  ½ teaspoon ground ginger
  ½ teaspoon ground nutmeg
   1 tablespoon butter or margarine
   1 tablespoon cornstarch
  ⅓ cup honey

Microwave Directions: Combine sweet potatoes and ⅓ cup orange juice in 2-quart microwave-safe baking dish; sprinkle with ginger and nutmeg. Dot with butter. Cover and microwave at HIGH (100%) 7 to 10 minutes or until sweet potatoes are tender, stirring halfway through cooking time. Combine cornstarch, remaining ⅓ cup orange juice and honey in medium microwave-safe bowl. Microwave at HIGH 2 minutes or until thickened, stirring every 30 seconds. Drain liquid from sweet potatoes; add to honey mixture. Microwave at HIGH 1 minute. Pour sauce over sweet potatoes and microwave at HIGH 1 minute more or until sweet potatoes are thoroughly heated.

Makes 4 servings

Favorite recipe from **National Honey Board**

Spicy Lemon Crescents

NUTMEG

Butternut Bisque

> 1 medium butternut squash (about 1½ pounds)
> 1 teaspoon margarine or butter
> 1 large onion, coarsely chopped (1 cup)
> 2 cans (about 14 ounces each) reduced-sodium or regular chicken broth, divided
> ½ teaspoon ground nutmeg or freshly grated nutmeg
> ⅛ teaspoon ground white pepper
> Plain nonfat yogurt and chives for garnish

Peel squash; cut flesh into ½-inch pieces. Set aside. Melt margarine in large saucepan over medium heat. Add onion. Cook and stir 3 minutes. Add squash and 1 can broth. Bring to a boil over high heat. Reduce heat to low. Cover and simmer 20 minutes or until squash is very tender.

Process squash mixture, in 2 batches, in food processor until smooth. Return soup to saucepan; add remaining can of broth, nutmeg and pepper. Simmer, uncovered, 5 minutes, stirring occasionally.*

Ladle soup into soup bowls. Place yogurt in pastry bag fitted with round decorating tip. Pipe onto soup in decorative design. Garnish with chives, if desired. *Makes about 5 cups (6 servings)*

*At this point, soup may be covered and refrigerated up to 2 days before serving. Reheat over medium heat, stirring occasionally.

Cream of Butternut Soup: *Add ½ cup whipping cream or half-and-half with second can of broth. Proceed as directed.*

Lemon-Nutmeg Spinach

> 1 box (10 ounces) BIRDS EYE® frozen Chopped or Whole Leaf Spinach
> 1½ tablespoons butter or margarine, melted
> 2 teaspoons lemon juice
> ⅛ teaspoon ground nutmeg

• Cook spinach according to package directions; drain well.

• Combine with remaining ingredients; toss to blend.

• Serve hot. *Makes 3 to 4 servings*

Prep Time: 3 to 4 minutes
Cook Time: 6 to 7 minutes

Butternut Bisque

OREGANO

Fish Creole

> 1 pound fresh or thawed frozen snapper or sole fillets
> 1 bag (16 ounces) **BIRDS EYE**® frozen Farm Fresh Mixtures Broccoli, Green Beans, Pearl Onions & Red Peppers
> 1 can (16 ounces) tomato sauce
> 1 tablespoon dried oregano or Italian seasoning
> 1 tablespoon vegetable oil
> 1½ teaspoons salt

- Preheat oven to 350°F.
- Place fish in 13×9-inch baking pan.
- In large bowl, combine vegetables, tomato sauce, oregano, oil and salt.
- Pour vegetable mixture over fish.
- Bake 20 minutes or until fish flakes easily when tested with fork.

Makes 4 servings

Tip: To remove fish odor from your hands after handling fish, rub your hands with salt and then wash them with cold water.

Prep Time: 5 minutes
Cook Time: 20 minutes

Black Olive Tapenade

> 1 can (6 ounces) pitted ripe olives, drained
> ¼ cup chopped red pepper
> 3 tablespoons olive oil
> 1 tablespoon lemon juice
> 1½ teaspoons dried oregano leaves
> ½ teaspoon minced garlic
> ½ cup (3 ounces) crumbled **ATHENOS**® Feta Natural Cheese

- **PLACE** all ingredients except cheese in blender or food processor container fitted with steel blade; cover. Process until smooth. Stir in cheese.
- **REFRIGERATE** several hours or overnight.
- **SERVE** with crackers or French bread chunks. Sprinkle with additional feta cheese, if desired.

Makes 1½ cups

Prep Time: 15 minutes plus refrigerating

---

spice note

To dry fresh oregano, tie the stems together and hang in a warm, well-ventilated place.

Fish Creole

OREGANO

Turkey Olé

½ cup minced onions
2 tablespoons butter or margarine
1 tablespoon all-purpose flour
1½ cups cubed cooked turkey
1½ cups prepared **HIDDEN VALLEY**® Original Ranch® Salad Dressing
3 ounces rotini (spiral macaroni), plain or spinach, cooked
½ (10-ounce) package frozen peas, thawed
⅓ cup canned diced green chiles, drained
⅛ to ¼ teaspoon black pepper (optional)
1 teaspoon dried oregano, crushed
3 tablespoons dry bread crumbs
1 tablespoon butter or margarine, melted
 Tomato wedges

Preheat oven to 350°F. In skillet, sauté onions in 2 tablespoons butter until tender. Stir in flour and cook until smooth and bubbly; remove from heat. In 1½-quart casserole, combine turkey, salad dressing, rotini, peas, chiles, pepper and oregano; stir in onions. In small bowl, combine bread crumbs with melted butter; sprinkle over casserole. Bake until heated through and bread crumbs are browned, 15 to 20 minutes. Garnish with tomato wedges.   *Makes 6 servings*

Herb-Sauced Pasta

2 cans (14½ ounces each) **CONTADINA**® Diced Tomatoes, undrained
2 tablespoons olive or vegetable oil
1 clove garlic, minced
½ teaspoon salt
¼ teaspoon crushed red pepper flakes
1 pound dry penne pasta
⅓ cup pine nuts, toasted
¼ cup chopped fresh basil *or* 1 tablespoon dried basil leaves, crushed
¼ cup chopped fresh oregano *or* 1 tablespoon dried oregano leaves, crushed
¼ cup chopped fresh parsley *or* 1 tablespoon dried parsley flakes, crushed
¼ cup chopped fresh thyme *or* 1 tablespoon dried thyme leaves, crushed
¼ teaspoon chopped fresh rosemary *or* dash of dried rosemary
¾ cup (3 ounces) grated Parmesan or Romano cheese

1. Combine tomatoes and juice, oil, garlic, salt and red pepper flakes in large saucepan. Bring to a boil. Reduce heat to low; simmer, uncovered, for 20 minutes, stirring occasionally.

2. Meanwhile, prepare pasta according to package directions; drain well.

3. Toss hot pasta with pine nuts and fresh herbs in large bowl. Add tomato mixture and cheese; toss until pasta is well coated. Serve hot or at room temperature.

Makes 8 servings

Prep Time: 5 minutes
Cook Time: 20 minutes

Easy Beef Tortilla Pizzas

> 1 **pound ground beef**
> 1 **medium onion, chopped**
> 1 **teaspoon dried oregano leaves, crushed**
> 1 **teaspoon salt**
> 4 **large flour tortillas (10-inch diameter)**
> 4 **teaspoons olive oil**
> 1 **medium tomato, seeded, chopped**
> **Greek or Mexican Topping (recipes follow)**

Cook and stir ground beef and onion in large nonstick skillet over medium heat or until beef is no longer pink, breaking up into ¾-inch crumbles. Pour off drippings. Sprinkle oregano and salt over beef, stirring to combine. Place tortillas on 2 large baking sheets. Lightly brush surface of each tortilla with oil. Bake in preheated 400°F oven 3 minutes. Divide beef mixture evenly over tops of tortillas; sprinkle tomato and desired topping over beef mixture. Bake at 400°F 12 to 14 minutes, rearranging baking sheets halfway through cooking time.

Makes 4 servings

Greek Topping: *Combine 1 teaspoon dried basil leaves, crushed, ½ teaspoon lemon pepper, 4 ounces crumbled feta cheese and ¼ cup grated Parmesan cheese in small bowl.*

Mexican Topping: *Combine 1 teaspoon dried cilantro, crushed, ½ teaspoon crushed dried red chilies, 1 cup (4 ounces) shredded Monterey Jack or Cheddar cheese and ⅓ cup sliced ripe olives in small bowl.*

Favorite recipe from **National Cattlemen's Beef Association**

OREGANO

Nonstick cooking spray
1¼ **pounds chicken tenders, cut crosswise in half**
1 **large tomato, cut into bite-size pieces**
½ **small cucumber, seeded, sliced**
½ **cup sweet onion slices (about 1 small)**
2 **tablespoons cider vinegar**
1 **tablespoon olive oil or vegetable oil**
3 **teaspoons minced fresh oregano or** ½ **teaspoon dried oregano leaves**
2 **teaspoons minced fresh mint or** ½ **teaspoon dried mint leaves**
¼ **teaspoon salt**
12 **lettuce leaves (optional)**
6 **whole wheat pita breads, cut crosswise in half**

1. Spray large nonstick skillet with cooking spray; heat over medium heat until hot. Add chicken; cook and stir 7 to 10 minutes or until browned and no longer pink in center. Cool slightly.

2. Combine chicken, tomato, cucumber and onion in medium bowl. Drizzle with vinegar and oil; toss to coat. Sprinkle with oregano, mint and salt; toss to combine.

3. Place 1 lettuce leaf in each pita bread half, if desired. Divide chicken mixture evenly; spoon into pita bread halves.   *Makes 6 servings*

Grilled Greek Chicken

1 **cup MIRACLE WHIP® Salad Dressing**
½ **cup chopped fresh parsley**
¼ **cup dry white wine or chicken broth**
1 **lemon, sliced and halved**
2 **tablespoons dried oregano leaves, crushed**
1 **tablespoon garlic powder**
1 **tablespoon black pepper**
2 **(2½- to 3-pound) broiler-fryers, cut up**

• Mix together all ingredients except chicken until well blended. Pour over chicken. Cover; marinate in refrigerator at least 20 minutes. Drain marinade; discard.

• Place chicken on grill over medium-hot coals (coals will have slight glow). Grill, covered, 20 to 25 minutes on each side or until tender.

Makes 8 servings

---

tasty tidbit

With its slightly hot, peppery flavor, oregano is found frequently in the cuisines of Italy, Greece, Mexico and Spain. Oregano enhances vinaigrettes, tomato-based sauces, poultry and meat dishes and grilled or roasted vegetables; it combines particularly well with garlic, thyme, parsley and olive oil.

Mediterranean Sandwich

PEPPER

Pepper Cheese Cocktail Puffs

½ package (17¼ ounces) frozen puff pastry, thawed
1 tablespoon Dijon mustard
½ cup (2 ounces) finely shredded Cheddar cheese
1 teaspoon cracked black pepper
1 egg
1 tablespoon water

1. Preheat oven to 400°F. Grease baking sheets.

2. Roll out 1 sheet puff pastry dough on well floured surface to 14×10-inch rectangle. Spread half of dough (from 10-inch side) with mustard. Sprinkle with cheese and pepper. Fold dough over filling; roll gently to seal edges.

3. Cut lengthwise into 3 strips; cut each strip diagonally into 1½-inch pieces. Place on prepared baking sheets. Beat egg and water in small bowl; brush on appetizers.

4. Bake appetizers 12 to 15 minutes or until puffed and deep golden brown. Remove from baking sheet to wire rack to cool.

Makes about 20 appetizers

Tip: Work quickly and efficiently when using puff pastry. The colder puff pastry is, the better it will puff in the hot oven. Also, this recipe can be easily doubled.

Prep and Bake Time: 30 minutes

Pepper Cheese Cocktail Puffs

109

PEPPER

Pepper is the dried berry of the Piper nigum plant family. Black peppercorn is the strongest and spiciest type; it is made from unripe berries fermented for several days before drying. White peppercorn, milder and less pungent, is made from fully ripe berries from which the outer hull has been removed. It is often used to add pepper flavor while avoiding the appearance of little black specks in light-colored dishes such as cream sauces, light soups, mayonnaise, etc.

Spinach Parmesan Risotto

3⅔ **cups reduced-sodium chicken broth**
½ **teaspoon ground white pepper**
  Nonstick cooking spray
1 **cup uncooked arborio rice**
1½ **cups chopped fresh spinach**
½ **cup fresh or frozen green peas**
1 **tablespoon minced fresh dill *or* 1 teaspoon dried dill weed**
½ **cup grated Parmesan cheese**
1 **teaspoon grated lemon peel**

1. Combine chicken broth and pepper in medium saucepan; cover. Bring to a simmer over medium-low heat. Keep broth simmering by adjusting heat.

2. Spray large saucepan with cooking spray; heat over medium-low heat until hot. Add rice; cook and stir 1 minute. Stir ⅔ cup hot chicken broth into saucepan; cook, stirring constantly, until broth is absorbed.

3. Stir remaining hot chicken broth into rice mixture, ½ cup at a time, stirring constantly until all broth is absorbed before adding next ½ cup. When last ½ cup chicken broth is added, stir spinach, peas and dill into saucepan. Cook, stirring gently until all broth is absorbed and rice is just tender but still firm to the bite. (Total cooking time for chicken broth absorption is about 35 to 40 minutes.)

4. Remove saucepan from heat; stir in cheese and lemon peel. Garnish as desired. *Makes 6 servings*

Note: *Arborio rice, an Italian-grown short-grain rice, has large, plump grains with a delicious nutty taste. It is traditionally used for risotto dishes because its high starch content produces a creamy texture.*

Lemon Pepper Marinade

⅔ **cup A.1.® Steak Sauce**
4 **teaspoons grated lemon peel**
1½ **teaspoons coarsely ground black pepper**

In small nonmetal bowl, combine steak sauce, lemon peel and pepper. Use to marinate beef, fish steak, poultry or pork for about 1 hour in the refrigerator.
Makes about ⅔ cup

Spinach Parmesan Risotto

Smoked Sausage with Cabbage and Sauerkraut

- ¼ pound **HILLSHIRE FARM**® **Bacon, diced**
- 1 **onion, sliced**
- 1 **carrot, diced**
- ½ **head cabbage, cut into quarters and thinly sliced**
- 1 **pound sauerkraut, drained**
- 1 **cup beer**
- ½ **cup beef broth**
- 2 **teaspoons black pepper**
- 1 **teaspoon caraway seeds**
- 4 **bay leaves**
- 1 **pound HILLSHIRE FARM**® **Smoked Sausage, cut into ¼-inch-thick slices**

Fry Bacon until crisp in Dutch oven over medium heat. Add onion and carrot. Cover and cook 5 minutes, stirring occasionally. Add cabbage; cover and cook 5 minutes or until cabbage is wilted, stirring frequently. Add sauerkraut, beer, beef broth, pepper, caraway and bay leaves. Bring to a boil; reduce heat to simmer. Cook, covered, 1 hour. Meanwhile, brown Smoked Sausage in small skillet over medium-high heat. Add sausage to cabbage mixture. Gently simmer 20 to 30 minutes. Serve hot. *Makes 6 servings*

Pepper-Cheese Bread

- 5½ **to 6 cups all-purpose flour**
- 2 **packages active dry yeast**
- 1 **cup milk**
- ⅔ **cup butter, cut into small pieces**
- 1 **tablespoon sugar**
- 1 **to 2 teaspoons coarsely ground black pepper**
- 1 **teaspoon salt**
- 4 **eggs**
- 2 **cups (8 ounces) shredded sharp Wisconsin Cheddar cheese**
- 1¼ **cups unseasoned mashed potatoes**

In large mixer bowl combine 2 cups flour and yeast. In small saucepan combine milk, butter, sugar, pepper and salt. Cook and stir until warm (115° to 120°F) and butter is almost melted. Add to flour mixture. Add eggs. Beat with electric mixer on low speed for 30 seconds, scraping side of bowl. Beat on high speed for 3 minutes. Stir in Cheddar cheese, mashed potatoes and as much remaining flour as can be mixed in with a spoon.

Turn out onto lightly floured surface. Knead 6 to 8 minutes or until dough is smooth and elastic, adding as much remaining flour as needed to make a moderately stiff dough. Shape into a ball. Place in greased bowl; turn once to grease surface. Cover; let rise in warm place (80° to 85°F) until double (about 1 hour).

Punch down dough; turn out onto lightly floured surface. Divide dough into 6 pieces. Cover; let rest 10 minutes. Roll each piece into 16-inch-long rope. On greased baking sheet braid 3 ropes together. Repeat on second greased baking sheet with remaining ropes. Cover; let rise in warm place until nearly doubled (about 30 minutes).

Preheat oven to 375°F. Bake 35 to 40 minutes or until golden brown, covering with foil the last 15 minutes of baking to prevent overbrowning. Remove from pans; cool.   *Makes 2 braids*

Prep Time: 50 minutes plus rising

Favorite recipe from **Wisconsin Milk Marketing Board**

Tuna with Peppercorns on a Bed of Greens

    4 **tuna steaks (about 1½ pounds)**
      Salt
    2 **teaspoons coarsely ground black pepper**
    1 **tablespoon butter or margarine**
    1 **large onion, thinly sliced**
    ¼ **cup dry white wine**
    ½ **pound fresh kale or spinach, washed**
    1 **tablespoon olive oil**
    ½ **teaspoon sugar**
    ¼ **teaspoon black pepper**
   12 **julienne strips carrot**
      Lemon slices and purple kale for garnish

Preheat oven to 325°F. Rinse tuna and pat dry with paper towels. Lightly sprinkle fish with salt, then press coarsely ground pepper into both sides of steaks; set aside.

Melt butter in large skillet over medium heat. Add onion; cook and stir 5 minutes or until crisp-tender. Add wine and remove from heat. Spread onion mixture on bottom of 13×9-inch glass baking dish. Top with fish. Bake 15 minutes. Spoon liquid over fish and bake 15 minutes more or until fish flakes easily when tested with fork.

Meanwhile, trim away tough stems from kale; cut leaves into 1-inch strips. Heat oil in medium skillet over medium-high heat. Add kale, sugar and black pepper. Cook and stir 2 to 3 minutes or until tender. Place kale on plates. Top with fish and onion mixture. Top fish with carrot strips. Garnish, if desired. Serve immediately.   *Makes 4 servings*

tasty tidbit

Red (cayenne) pepper, chili pepper, bell pepper and paprika are all fruits from the capsicum family and are not related to black and white pepper.

Zesty Peppered Steaks

4 ounces light cream cheese
½ cup A.1.® Original or A.1.® Bold & Spicy Steak Sauce, divided
1 tablespoon prepared horseradish
4 (4-ounce) beef rib eye steaks, about ¾ inch thick
2 teaspoons coarsely ground black pepper

In small saucepan, over medium heat, stir cream cheese, ¼ cup steak sauce and horseradish until heated through; keep warm.

Brush both sides of steaks with 2 tablespoons steak sauce, dividing evenly. Sprinkle ¼ teaspoon pepper on each side of each steak, pressing into meat and sauce. Grill steaks over medium-high heat or broil 4 inches from heat source 4 minutes on each side or to desired doneness, basting occasionally with remaining 2 tablespoons steak sauce. Serve with warm sauce. Garnish as desired.

Makes 4 servings

Creole Macaroni and Cheese

½ cup butter or margarine
1 package (12 ounces) elbow macaroni
1 can (14½ ounces) DEL MONTE® Diced Tomatoes with Garlic & Onion
1 teaspoon salt
½ teaspoon white pepper
1 tablespoon all-purpose flour
1 can (12 fluid ounces) evaporated milk
2 cups shredded sharp Cheddar cheese

1. Melt butter in large skillet. Add macaroni, tomatoes, salt and pepper. Cook 5 minutes, stirring occasionally.

2. Add 1½ cups water; bring to boil. Cover and simmer 20 minutes or until macaroni is tender.

3. Sprinkle in flour; blend well. Stir in evaporated milk and cheese. Simmer 5 minutes, stirring occasionally, until cheese is completely melted. Garnish with green pepper or parsley, if desired. Serve immediately.

Makes 4 to 6 servings

Prep and Cook Time: 35 minutes

Zesty Peppered Steak

PEPPER

Hot and Sour Soup

- 3 cans (about 14 ounces each) chicken broth
- 8 ounces boneless skinless chicken breasts, cut into ¼-inch-thick strips
- 1 cup shredded carrots
- 1 cup thinly sliced mushrooms
- ½ cup bamboo shoots, cut into matchstick-size strips
- 2 tablespoons rice vinegar or white wine vinegar
- ½ to ¾ teaspoon white pepper
- ¼ to ½ teaspoon hot pepper sauce
- 2 tablespoons cornstarch
- 2 tablespoons soy sauce
- 1 tablespoon dry sherry
- 2 medium green onions, sliced
- 1 egg, slightly beaten

Combine chicken broth, chicken, carrots, mushrooms, bamboo shoots, vinegar, pepper and hot pepper sauce in large saucepan. Bring to a boil over medium-high heat; reduce heat to low. Cover and simmer about 5 minutes or until chicken is no longer pink in center.

Stir together cornstarch, soy sauce and sherry in small bowl until smooth. Add to chicken broth mixture. Cook and stir until mixture comes to a boil. Stir in green onions and egg. Cook about 1 minute, stirring in one direction, until egg is cooked. Ladle soup into bowls.

Makes about 7 cups or 6 side-dish servings

Red Cabbage Salad

- 1 cup WESSON® Best Blend Oil
- 1 cup cider vinegar
- 1 cup seasoned rice vinegar
- ⅔ cup sugar
- 1½ tablespoons chopped fresh dill weed or 1 teaspoon dried dill weed
- 1 tablespoon celery seed
- 2 teaspoons coarsely ground black pepper
- 2 teaspoons salt
- 2 to 2½ pounds red cabbage, shredded

Combine *all* ingredients *except* cabbage; mix until sugar is dissolved. Place cabbage in large bowl and pour dressing over cabbage; toss until completely coated. Cover and refrigerate at least 6 hours or up to 24 hours, tossing salad several times. Toss once before serving. *Makes 3 quarts salad*

Hot and Sour Soup

PEPPER

tasty tidbit

If possible, use a pepper grinder or mortar and pestle to grind pepper as you need it for cooking—the taste is far superior to that of preground pepper, which loses its flavor very quickly.

Pesto-Cheese Logs

⅓ **cup walnuts**
1 **package (8 ounces) cream cheese, softened**
⅓ **cup prepared pesto sauce**
⅓ **cup crumbled feta cheese**
2 **teaspoons cracked black pepper**
2 **tablespoons finely shredded carrot**
2 **tablespoons chopped fresh parsley**
Assorted crackers
Carrot slivers, parsley and fresh thyme for garnish

Preheat oven to 350°F. To toast walnuts, place on baking sheet. Bake 8 to 10 minutes or until golden brown, stirring frequently; cool. Process walnuts in food processor using on/off pulsing action until walnuts are ground, but not pasty. Remove from food processor; set aside.

Process cream cheese, pesto and feta cheese in food processor until smooth. Spread ¾ cup cheese mixture on waxed paper and form 4-inch log. Wrap waxed paper around cheese log. Repeat with remaining cheese mixture. Refrigerate logs at least 4 hours, until well chilled. Roll each chilled log to form 5-inch log.

Combine walnuts and pepper. Roll 1 log in nut mixture to coat. Combine carrot and parsley. Roll remaining log in carrot mixture to coat. Serve immediately or wrap and refrigerate up to a day before serving. To serve, thinly slice log and serve with crackers. Garnish, if desired. *Makes 2 logs*

Cheddar Pepper Muffins

2 **cups all-purpose flour**
1 **tablespoon sugar**
1 **tablespoon baking powder**
1 **teaspoon coarsely ground black pepper**
½ **teaspoon salt**
1¼ **cups milk**
¼ **cup vegetable oil**
1 **egg**
1 **cup (4 ounces) shredded sharp Cheddar cheese, divided**

Preheat oven to 400°F. Generously grease or paper-line 12 (2½-inch) muffin cups. Combine flour, sugar, baking powder, pepper and salt in large bowl. Combine milk, oil and egg until blended in small bowl. Stir into flour mixture just until moistened. Fold in ¾ cup cheese. Spoon into muffin cups. Sprinkle with remaining cheese. Bake 15 to 20 minutes or until light golden brown. Cool in pan on wire rack 5 minutes. Remove from pan; serve warm. *Makes 12 muffins*

Pesto-Cheese Logs

119

ROSEMARY

Mesquite Turkey Kabobs with Fresh Rosemary

1½ cups LAWRY'S® Mesquite Marinade with Lime Juice, divided
1¼ pounds turkey cutlets, cut into 2½×1-inch strips
½ ounce fresh rosemary, cut into 1-inch sprigs
1 yellow bell pepper, cut into chunks
1 red bell pepper, cut into chunks
1 red onion, cut into thin wedges
Skewers

In large resealable plastic food storage bag, combine 1 cup Mesquite Marinade and turkey; seal bag. Marinate in refrigerator at least 30 minutes. Remove turkey; discard used marinade. Place rosemary sprig in center of each turkey piece; fold turkey in half, enclosing rosemary sprig. Alternately thread turkey, bell peppers and onion onto skewers. Grill or broil skewers 10 to 15 minutes or until turkey is no longer pink in center and juices run clear when cut, turning once and basting often with additional ½ cup Mesquite Marinade. *Do not baste during last 5 minutes of cooking.* Discard any remaining marinade.   ***Makes 4 servings***

Serving Suggestion: *Serve over bed of herbed brown rice with a tossed green salad.*

120

Mesquite Turkey Kabobs with Fresh Rosemary

ROSEMARY

2 tablespoons olive oil
1 clove garlic, minced
2 teaspoons snipped fresh rosemary leaves
1½ pounds red skin potatoes, unpeeled and cut into ½-inch cubes
½ teaspoon salt
½ teaspoon black pepper
Fresh rosemary sprig and tomato wedges (optional)

Heat oil in large skillet over medium heat until hot. Add garlic and snipped rosemary; cook and stir 2 minutes. Add potatoes, salt and pepper. Cook 5 minutes, stirring occasionally. Reduce heat to medium-low; cook, uncovered, about 20 minutes or until potatoes are golden brown and crisp, turning occasionally. Garnish with rosemary sprig and tomato, if desired. Serve hot. Refrigerate leftovers. *Makes 4 to 6 side-dish servings*

Favorite recipe from **Bob Evans**®

Rotisserie Chicken with Pesto Brush

2 BUTTERBALL® Fresh Young Roasters
¼ cup chopped fresh oregano
¼ cup chopped fresh parsley
2 tablespoons chopped fresh rosemary
2 tablespoons chopped fresh thyme
½ cup olive oil
½ cup balsamic vinegar

Combine oregano, parsley, rosemary, thyme, oil and vinegar in small bowl. Roast chicken according to rotisserie directions. Dip brush into herb mixture; brush chicken with herb mixture every 30 minutes for first 2 hours of roasting. Brush every 15 minutes during last hour of roasting. Roast chicken until internal temperature reaches 180°F in thigh and meat is no longer pink.

Makes 16 servings

Tip: *To make an aromatic herb brush, bundle sprigs of rosemary, thyme, oregano and parsley together. Tie bundle with kitchen string. Use as brush for pesto.*

Prep Time: 15 minutes plus roasting time

tasty tidbit

When using dried rosemary leaves, crush them just before using. Fresh leaves should be finely chopped or crushed in a mortar and pestle because their texture is somewhat tough. Whole sprigs of fresh rosemary can be used in long-cooking dishes; remove the sprigs before serving.

Rosemary Hash Potatoes

123

ROSEMARY

Rosemary Chicken with Asparagus Lemon Rice

¼ **cup dry white wine**
3 **cloves garlic, minced**
1 **tablespoon finely chopped fresh rosemary**
1 **tablespoon vegetable oil**
1 **tablespoon low-sodium soy sauce**
1 **teaspoon sugar**
½ **teaspoon ground black pepper**
6 **boneless, skinless chicken breast halves (about 2¼ pounds)**
  Vegetable cooking spray
3 **cups cooked rice (cooked in low-sodium chicken broth)**
10 **spears asparagus, blanched and cut into 1-inch pieces (¼ pound)**
1 **teaspoon grated lemon peel**
1 **teaspoon lemon pepper**
½ **teaspoon salt**
  Lemon slices for garnish
  Fresh rosemary sprigs for garnish

Combine wine, garlic, rosemary, oil, soy sauce, sugar and pepper in large shallow glass dish. Add chicken, turning to coat; cover and marinate in refrigerator at least 1 hour. Heat large skillet coated with cooking spray over medium-high heat until hot. Add chicken and marinade; cook 7 minutes on each side or until brown and no longer pink in center. Combine rice, asparagus, lemon peel, lemon pepper and salt in large bowl. To serve, spoon rice on individual serving plates. Cut chicken into strips; fan over rice. Garnish with lemon and rosemary.   *Makes 6 servings*

Favorite recipe from **USA Rice Federation**

Rosemary Breadsticks

⅔ **cup 2% reduced-fat milk**
¼ **cup finely chopped fresh chives**
2 **teaspoons baking powder**
1 **teaspoon finely chopped fresh rosemary or dried rosemary**
¾ **teaspoon salt**
½ **teaspoon ground black pepper**
¾ **cup whole wheat flour**
¾ **cup all-purpose flour**
  Nonstick cooking spray

1. Combine milk, chives, baking powder, rosemary, salt and pepper in large bowl; mix well. Stir in flours, ½ cup at a time, until blended. Turn onto floured surface and knead dough about 5 minutes or until smooth and elastic, adding more flour if dough is sticky. Let stand 30 minutes at room temperature.

2. Preheat oven to 375°F. Spray baking sheet with cooking spray. Divide dough into 12 equal balls, about 1¼ ounces each. Roll each ball into long thin rope and place on prepared baking sheet. Lightly spray breadsticks with cooking spray. Bake about 12 minutes or until bottoms are golden brown. Turn breadsticks over and bake about 10 minutes more or until golden brown.

Makes 12 breadsticks

Grilled Ratatouille Sandwich

⅓ **cup olive oil**
⅓ **cup FRENCH'S® Deli Brown Mustard**
 1 **tablespoon chopped fresh rosemary *or* 1 teaspoon dried rosemary**
 3 **cloves garlic, minced**
½ **cup kalamata olives, pitted and chopped**
½ **of a small eggplant (about ¾ pound)**
 1 **medium zucchini**
 1 **large red onion**
 2 **large ripe plum tomatoes**
 1 **large red bell pepper**
 1 **(12-inch) sourdough baguette, cut lengthwise in half (about 12 ounces)**

1. Combine oil, mustard, rosemary and garlic in small bowl. Place olives in food processor; add 2 tablespoons mustard mixture. Cover and process until smooth; set aside. Reserve remaining mustard mixture.

2. Cut eggplant and zucchini lengthwise into ¼-inch-thick slices. Cut onion and tomatoes crosswise into ½-inch-thick slices. Cut red bell pepper lengthwise into 2-inch-wide pieces; discard seeds. Place vegetables on platter. Baste with reserved mustard mixture.

3. Place vegetables on oiled grid or vegetable basket. Grill over medium-high heat 3 to 5 minutes or until vegetables are tender, basting and turning once.

4. To serve, remove and discard excess bread from bread halves. Spread olive mixture on cut surfaces of bread. Layer vegetables on bottom half of bread; cover with top half. Cut crosswise into 4 portions. *Makes 4 servings*

Prep Time: 25 minutes
Cook Time: 5 minutes

ROSEMARY

Rosemary Steak

4 boneless top loin beef steaks or New York strip steaks (about 6 ounces each)
2 tablespoons minced fresh rosemary
2 cloves garlic, minced
1 tablespoon extra-virgin olive oil
1 teaspoon grated lemon peel
1 teaspoon coarsely ground black pepper
½ teaspoon salt
Fresh rosemary sprigs

Score steaks in diamond pattern on both sides. Combine minced rosemary, garlic, oil, lemon peel, pepper and salt in small bowl; rub mixture onto surface of meat. Cover and refrigerate at least 15 minutes. Grill steaks over medium-hot KINGSFORD® Briquets about 4 minutes per side until medium-rare or to desired doneness. Cut steaks diagonally into ½-inch-thick slices. Garnish with rosemary sprigs. *Makes 4 servings*

Savory Rosemary Quick Bread

1¾ cups reduced-fat buttermilk baking mix
1 cup (4 ounces) shredded Cheddar cheese, divided
¾ cup skim milk
2 egg whites
1⅓ cups FRENCH'S® French Fried Onions, divided
1 tablespoon sugar
1 tablespoon butter, melted
2 teaspoons chopped fresh rosemary or ½ teaspoon dried rosemary

Preheat oven to 375°F. Line 9-inch square baking pan with foil; spray with nonstick cooking spray.

Combine baking mix, ½ cup cheese, milk, egg whites, ⅔ cup French Fried Onions, sugar, butter and rosemary in large bowl; stir just until moistened. Do not overmix. Spread into prepared pan.

Bake 20 minutes or until toothpick inserted in center comes out clean. Sprinkle with remaining cheese and ⅔ cup onions. Bake 1 minute or until cheese is melted and onions are golden. Remove to wire rack; cool 5 minutes. Remove foil. Cut into squares. Serve warm or cool. *Makes 8 servings*

Prep Time: 15 minutes
Cook Time: 21 minutes

Rosemary Steak

127

ROSEMARY

tasty tidbit

Use rosemary sprigs as a grilling brush, so that the meat or poultry and the oil or butter used for basting are all infused with a wonderful rosemary scent. Or, add several rosemary sprigs to the coals during the last 10 minutes of cooking.

Savory Chicken and Biscuits

- 1 **pound boneless, skinless chicken thighs or breasts, cut into 1-inch pieces**
- 1 **medium potato, cut into 1-inch pieces**
- 1 **medium yellow onion, cut into 1-inch pieces**
- 8 **ounces fresh mushrooms, quartered**
- 1 **cup fresh baby carrots**
- 1 **cup chopped celery**
- 1 **(14½-ounce) can chicken broth**
- 3 **cloves garlic, minced**
- 1 **teaspoon dried rosemary leaves**
- 1 **teaspoon salt**
- 1 **teaspoon black pepper**
- 3 **tablespoons cornstarch blended with ½ cup cold water**
- 1 **cup frozen peas, thawed**
- 1 **(4-ounce) jar sliced pimentos, drained**
- 1 **package BOB EVANS® Frozen Buttermilk Biscuit Dough**

Preheat oven to 375°F. Combine chicken, potato, onion, mushrooms, carrots, celery, broth, garlic, rosemary, salt and pepper in large saucepan. Bring to a boil over high heat. Reduce heat to low and simmer, uncovered, 5 minutes. Stir in cornstarch mixture; cook 2 minutes. Stir in peas and pimentos; return to a boil. Transfer chicken mixture to 2-quart casserole dish; arrange frozen biscuits on top. Bake 30 to 35 minutes or until biscuits are golden brown. Refrigerate leftovers. *Makes 4 to 6 servings*

Rosemary Garlic Rub

- 2 **tablespoons chopped fresh rosemary**
- 1½ **teaspoons LAWRY'S® Seasoned Salt**
- 1 **teaspoon LAWRY'S® Garlic Pepper**
- ½ **teaspoon LAWRY'S® Garlic Powder with Parsley**
- 1 **pound top sirloin steak**
- 1 **tablespoon olive oil**

In small bowl, combine rosemary, Seasoned Salt, Garlic Pepper and Garlic Powder with Parsley; mix well. Brush both sides of steak with oil. Sprinkle with herb mixture, pressing onto steak. Grill or broil steak 15 to 20 minutes or until desired doneness, turning halfway through grilling time. *Makes 4 servings*

Serving Suggestion: *Serve with oven-roasted or french-fried potatoes and honey-coated carrots.*

Hint: *This rub is also great on lamb or pork.*

Savory Chicken and Biscuits

THYME

Roasted Herb & Garlic Tenderloin

1 well-trimmed beef tenderloin roast (3 to 4 pounds)
1 tablespoon black peppercorns
2 tablespoons chopped fresh basil *or* 2 teaspoons dried basil leaves, crushed
4½ teaspoons chopped fresh thyme *or* 1½ teaspoons dried thyme leaves, crushed
1 tablespoon chopped fresh rosemary *or* 1 teaspoon dried rosemary, crushed
1 tablespoon minced garlic
Salt and black pepper (optional)

1. Preheat oven to 425°F. To hold shape of roast, tie roast with cotton string in 1½-inch intervals.

2. Place peppercorns in small heavy resealable plastic food storage bag. Squeeze out excess air; seal bag tightly. Pound peppercorns with flat side of meat mallet or rolling pin until cracked.

3. Place roast on meat rack in shallow roasting pan. Combine cracked peppercorns, basil, thyme, rosemary and garlic in small bowl; rub over top surface of roast.

4. Insert meat thermometer into thickest part of roast. Roast in oven 40 to 50 minutes or until thermometer registers 125° to 130°F for rare or 135° to 145°F for medium-rare, depending on thickness of roast.

5. Transfer roast to carving board; tent with foil. Let stand 10 minutes before carving. Remove and discard string. To serve, carve crosswise into ½-inch-thick slices with large carving knife. Season with salt and pepper.

Makes 10 to 12 servings

Roasted Herb & Garlic Tenderloin

THYME

Thyme-Cheese Bubble Loaf

1 **package active dry yeast**
1 **teaspoon sugar**
1 **cup warm water, 105° to 115°F**
3 **cups all-purpose flour**
1 **teaspoon salt**
2 **tablespoons vegetable oil**
1 **cup shredded Monterey Jack cheese (4 ounces)**
4 **tablespoons butter or margarine, melted**
¼ **cup chopped parsley**
3 **teaspoons finely chopped fresh thyme or ¾ teaspoon dried thyme leaves, crushed**

1. To proof yeast, sprinkle yeast and sugar over warm water in small bowl; stir until yeast is dissolved. Let stand 5 minutes or until mixture is bubbly.

2. Combine flour and salt in food processor. With food processor running, add yeast mixture and oil. Process until mixture forms dough that leaves side of bowl. If dough is too dry, add 1 to 2 tablespoons water. If dough is too wet, add 1 to 2 tablespoons additional flour until dough leaves side of bowl. Dough will be sticky.

3. Place dough in large greased bowl. Turn dough over so that top is greased. Cover with towel; let rise in warm place about 1 hour or until doubled in bulk.

4. Punch down dough. Knead cheese into dough on lightly floured surface until evenly distributed. Cover with towel; let rest 10 minutes.

5. Grease 1½-quart casserole dish or 8½×4½-inch loaf pan; set aside. Combine butter, parsley and thyme in small bowl.

6. Roll out dough into 8×6-inch rectangle with lightly floured rolling pin. Cut dough into 48 (1-inch) squares with pizza cutter. Shape each square into a ball. Dip into parsley mixture. Place in prepared pan.

7. Cover with towel; let rise in warm place about 45 minutes or until doubled in bulk. Preheat oven to 375°F.

8. Bake 35 to 40 minutes or until top is golden and loaf sounds hollow when tapped. Immediately remove from casserole dish; cool on wire rack 30 minutes. Serve warm. Store leftover bread in refrigerator. *Makes 1 loaf*

Thyme-Cheese Bubble Loaf

THYME

Warm Lemon & Thyme Potato Salad

2 pounds red potatoes, scrubbed and cut into ¼-inch slices
2 cloves garlic, minced
¼ cup olive oil
2 tablespoons bottled or fresh lemon juice
1 teaspoon dried thyme leaves or 2 tablespoons chopped fresh thyme
Romaine lettuce leaves

1. Bring water in large saucepan to a boil over high heat. Add potato slices. Reduce heat to medium-low. Simmer, covered, 10 minutes or until potatoes are barely tender. Pour potatoes into colander; drain well.

2. Cook garlic in oil in large deep skillet over medium heat 1 to 2 minutes. Stir in lemon juice and thyme; heat through. Add drained potatoes; stir lightly to coat potatoes with dressing. Season with salt and pepper. Reduce heat to medium-low. Cover and cook 4 to 5 minutes, turning once.

3. Arrange lettuce on 6 salad plates; top with hot potato mixture.

Makes 6 servings

Hidden Herb Grilled Turkey Breast

1 (3- to 9-pound) BUTTERBALL® Breast of Young Turkey, thawed
¼ cup coarsely chopped fresh parsley
2 tablespoons chopped mixed fresh herbs such as thyme, oregano and marjoram
2 tablespoons grated Parmesan cheese
1 teaspoon olive oil
½ teaspoon lemon juice
½ teaspoon salt
¼ teaspoon garlic powder
¼ teaspoon black pepper
Vegetable oil

Prepare grill for indirect-heat grilling. Combine parsley, herbs, Parmesan cheese, oil, lemon juice, salt, garlic powder and pepper in medium bowl. Gently loosen and lift turkey skin from surface of meat. Spread herb blend evenly over breast meat. Replace skin over herb blend. Brush skin with vegetable oil. Place turkey breast skin side up on prepared grill. Cover grill and cook 1½ to 2½ hours for a 3- to 9-pound breast or until internal temperature reaches 170°F and meat is no longer pink in center. *Number of servings varies*

Prep Time: 15 minutes plus grilling time

ACKNOWLEDGMENTS

The publishers would like to thank the companies and organizations listed below for the use of their recipes and photographs in this publication.

A.1.® Steak Sauce

Birds Eye®

Bob Evans®

Butterball® Turkey Company

Del Monte Corporation

Dole Food Company, Inc.

Duncan Hines® brand is a registered trademark of Aurora Foods Inc.

Filippo Berio Olive Oil

Golden Grain®

Grey Poupon® Mustard

Hershey Foods Corporation

Hillshire Farm®

Hunt-Wesson, Inc.

The HV Company

Kikkoman International Inc.

The Kingsford Products Company

Kraft Foods, Inc.

Land O' Lakes, Inc.

Lawry's® Foods, Inc.

Lipton®

M&M/MARS

McIlhenny Company (TABASCO® brand Pepper Sauce)

National Cattlemen's Beef Association

National Chicken Council

National Honey Board

National Turkey Federation

Newman's Own, Inc.®

The Quaker® Kitchens

Reckitt & Colman Inc.

Sargento® Foods Inc.

The J.M. Smucker Company

Sonoma® Dried Tomatoes

The Sugar Association, Inc.

Uncle Ben's Inc.

USA Rice Federation

Wisconsin Milk Marketing Board

INDEX

METRIC CONVERSION CHART

VOLUME MEASUREMENTS (dry)

⅛ teaspoon	0.5 mL
¼ teaspoon	1 mL
½ teaspoon	2 mL
¾ teaspoon	4 mL
1 teaspoon	5 mL
1 tablespoon	15 mL
2 tablespoons	30 mL
¼ cup	60 mL
⅓ cup	75 mL
½ cup	125 mL
⅔ cup	150 mL
¾ cup	175 mL
1 cup	250 mL
2 cups = 1 pint	500 mL
3 cups	750 mL
4 cups = 1 quart	1 L

VOLUME MEASUREMENTS (fluid)

1 fluid ounce (2 tablespoons)	30 mL
4 fluid ounces (½ cup)	125 mL
8 fluid ounces (1 cup)	250 mL
12 fluid ounces (1½ cups)	375 mL
16 fluid ounces (2 cups)	500 mL

WEIGHTS (mass)

½ ounce	15 g
1 ounce	30 g
3 ounces	90 g
4 ounces	120 g
8 ounces	225 g
10 ounces	285 g
12 ounces	360 g
16 ounces = 1 pound	450 g

DIMENSIONS

1/16 inch	2 mm
⅛ inch	3 mm
¼ inch	6 mm
½ inch	1.5 cm
¾ inch	2 cm
1 inch	2.5 cm

OVEN TEMPERATURES

250°F	120°C
275°F	140°C
300°F	150°C
325°F	160°C
350°F	180°C
375°F	190°C
400°F	200°C
425°F	220°C
450°F	230°C

BAKING PAN SIZES

Utensil	Size in Inches/Quarts	Metric Volume	Size in Centimeters
Baking or Cake Pan (square or rectangular)	8 × 8 × 2	2 L	20 × 20 × 5
	9 × 9 × 2	2.5 L	23 × 23 × 5
	12 × 8 × 2	3 L	30 × 20 × 5
	13 × 9 × 2	3.5 L	33 × 23 × 5
Loaf Pan	8 × 4 × 3	1.5 L	20 × 10 × 7
	9 × 5 × 3	2 L	23 × 13 × 7
Round Layer Cake Pan	8 × 1½	1.2 L	20 × 4
	9 × 1½	1.5 L	23 × 4
Pie Plate	8 × 1¼	750 mL	20 × 3
	9 × 1¼	1 L	23 × 3
Baking Dish or Casserole	1 quart	1 L	—
	1½ quart	1.5 L	—
	2 quart	2 L	—